CASSANDRA ELLIS

CLOTH

30+ Beautiful Projects to Sew from Linen, Cotton, Silk, Wool, and Hide

Photography by Catherine Gratwicke

STC Craft | A Melanie Falick Book

New York

Contents

Everything Has A Story

I've always been defined by the cloth that I wear (usually black and often silk) as well as by my various careers over the years, as designer, event organizer, maker, seller, and writer. How my home feels is all about my love of cloth. It is spare but tactile and I, or other artisans, have made every textile item. The fabrics are old or handmade and, of course, everything has a story, because I thrive on back-stories. I have always loved fabric and fabric stores and I've always been compelled to make things. Touch—in this case, handling things—has always been my most pronounced sense. I am the picker-upper, the stroker, and the crumpler of cloth—perhaps a fabric store owner's worst nightmare!

I have sewn since I was a child—dolls' clothes, an award-winning nativity scene (still very proud) and the curtains for my playhouse. I'm sure they were pretty rough in finish but the making was very fulfilling. The teenage years were more expressive and the sewing a little better (and this is where my love affair with black began).

Although I dreamed of studying fashion and design at college, I didn't go—economics and business got me instead. All the while I was making, thinking, creating. I am fanatical about certain designers and interiors stores, but have never been that interested in crafts. I can guarantee that I will never make a quilted finger puppet, but I will always make quilts. I like to think of it as mindful making. I've always wanted to live by William Morris's well-known ethos: "Have nothing in your house that you do not know to be useful, or believe to be beautiful" and I hope now that I do. A few years ago I realized that making is thinking. To make useful and beautiful objects requires more than just making on its own—it is an emotive process and continues my story and the stories of those I make for now.

I am immersed in thought when deep in a commission and slightly obsessed with the cultural aspect of fabric. How communities grow, shrink, or disappear and how new communities are made is gripping stuff. Of course, any story involving cloth and making is completely compelling. I love books on making as much as I like a romp through Thoreau and, somehow, the two aspects combine perfectly.

Most of all, I know that we are all born to make—I make, therefore I am. For me, it's still usually black or muted in color, although the stitching is much better. Japanese kimono silk is still my personal favorite cloth, followed very closely by silk, velvet, and leather (oh, and hemp). You won't find many bright colors in my making, but I do love looking at them. I still watch Dries Van Noten catwalk shows obsessively, but mostly I am happiest in a fabric store, looking, thinking, and crumpling.

He wishes for the Cloths of Heaven

Had I the heavens' embroidered cloths,
Enwrought with golden and silver light,
The blue and the dim and the dark cloths
Of night and light and the half-light,
I would spread the cloths under your feet:
But I, being poor, have only my dreams;
I have spread my dreams under your feet;
Tread softly because you tread on my dreams.

WILLIAM BUTLER YEATS

Whether it is a bolt of liquid silk, a rough antique feedsack, or an Indian cotton ralli quilt, cloth moves us. Its tactility and three-dimensional nature seems to bring out a passion in everyone. We hunt and gather precious pieces and scraps without knowing what to do with them, but have them we must. Sometimes, we buy a piece of fabric just because of the way it looks, sometimes because it captures a memory as heady as any photograph or postcard. Each piece may have emotional or historical significance; it may be new but special, or something made in an ethically sound way.

As well as being emotionally evocative, cloth is a tactile delight—and when we touch, we feel. You instantly know the difference between silk and polyester through your fingertips—it almost feels like you can touch the maker's hand within natural cloth. Not matter how hard technology tries, man-made fibers cannot truly replicate the feel of handmade textiles. Touch connects us—it is the first sense we develop as a baby and is always engaged when buying fabric. Our eyes may fool us, but our hands can't deceive. Everyone (including animals) loves natural materials. From babies wrapped in sheepskins to cashmere shawls draped around our grandmothers' shoulders, each stage of life is enveloped in a fabric made of natural fibers that is full of tactile promise.

Scraps of cloth can give you clues about a different life or place—and, in that way, transport you to somewhere else. Travels to distant shores or local markets can provide a cornucopia of visual and tactile delights. You may be shopping with a purpose, or a piece of cloth can just speak to you. It can change everything—how you look and how you live. It can be the starting point for a quilt, a room, or the way you dress. Cloth is also a storyteller. It speaks of travels near and far, people you've loved, and some you've lost. It talks of huge life choices and sometimes just a simple, lovely shopping experience. Cloth can also open up the world to you. Every continent and most countries have their own unique textile history. From the khadi cotton of India to the linen of Ireland, you'll find more stories, more history, and many hands in the making. We are globally connected through the fabric that we can now buy and use. You can mix Moroccan wool rugs with a mud-cloth-upholstered chair and a kimono silk quilt and top it off with a pillow crafted from suede.

Cloth has been made and loved for centuries. The antique and vintage textile industry is booming, as there is nothing more thrilling than finding aged French ribbons or a vintage Welsh blanket. You can buy at stores, markets, and fairs, or even online if you're prepared to risk using only one sense. Whether you're upcycling or just enjoying the handmade beauty of these goods, they are waiting to be used to create something beautiful for you and your home, or just to be admired for what they are.

Fabric has been used as currency (and, in some places, still is) as well as packaging for food and other goods—for instance, linen feedsacks to hold grains and cotton sacks to hold sugar and flour. It has visually defined the difference between rich and poor, and has provided the route to commercial riches through industrialization. It has made countries specialists in their field and has crippled others by the same process of industrialization. Some nations, such as India, have been reborn politically through producing their own cloth, while other third-world countries have been literally sickened by the demand for cotton. On the upside, many textile industries that have been in steady decline are now being rejuvenated through young entrepreneurs and investment in craft skills rather than mass production. Fabrics that were almost lost are now valued once again. It's an exciting time, when old traditions and a new set of skills are coming together to lift fabric production back up as an artisanal industry.

Fabric is a material that we can all make something with. It doesn't require advanced skills or training like woodwork or gilding—which is a bonus—but it shouldn't be relegated to a lesser state just because we can all engage with it. It wasn't long ago that everyone made textile goods—quilts, clothing, and all sorts of other things—from necessity as well as desire. Working with fabric was an intrinsic part of life.

Mindful making has the potential to enrich all our lives. When we make something for our homes or clothes with care and consideration, we are able to experience the contemplative pleasures of creating by hand. So when you make, enjoy the process, don't hurry it, and try not to "bash it out," but take pride in what you can create.

Last, but not least, textiles add the final ingredient (the sixth sense, if you like) to rooms and homes—which otherwise can appear (and feel) cold and lifeless. Think not just of pillows (although these are great for bringing in color and pattern), but also of rugs and throws and blankets, too. Choose the fabric for your furniture carefully, as you will sit or lie on it for many years—you want it to feel great and look good.

Mix your travel finds with your vintage and your handmade textiles to create a physically and emotionally layered home, a home that tells your story through your hands and heart, as well as the hands and lives of others.

I hope you find *Cloth* is both a resource and an opportunity for you to create beautiful and useful things for you and your home. These projects are just a handful of hundreds of ideas and uses for cloth. All of them can be adjusted to fit either your aesthetic or your overwhelming fabric stash—or both.

Cloth is a personal guide to cotton, wool, silk, hide, and linen. One book alone cannot hope to tell and show you everything, but I hope that through the projects, a few facts and figures, and the stories of makers and nations, cloth will come to life for you through your eyes and your hands.

Toolkit

A sewer's toolkit is a very pleasurable thing. Many of the tools you need can be used for most making pursuits and you may already own them. But some are specifically created and beautifully designed just for one project.

There are essential items, which (I think) you must have, then there are the extra bits and bobs, nice things, indulgent things, more excuses to stand in a haberdashery store things. . .

Sewing Machine

The key to the right sewing machine is research and a bit of forward planning. What are you going to use your sewing machine for? Are you planning on launching an accessories empire or are you more likely to make a quilt, a few lovely aprons, a bag, and do a bit of mending each year? Sewing machines vary from $80–$4,500 plus, so make sure you don't under- or overspend (trust me from my own experience on this). It's important to choose a respected and well-known brand, firstly, because it will always come with a decent warranty and, secondly, because you will always find replacement parts and accessories easily. Each brand is slightly different, a little bit like cars, so it is important to find a brand that you like. Visit a specialist sewing center or department store with a proper sewing section—they will have sewing enthusiasts who can show you how to use a machine and you can try out different brands. If you can, have a lesson on the machine you want to buy so that you can get used to it—your sewing machine will become your friend if you know it and treat it well. My Brother machine has traveled the globe with me and I know its quirks and foibles inside out. I know what it can and can't do and when it needs attention.

The majority of sewers only use straight or zigzag stitch, so a basic, sturdy machine from a well-known brand will suit most people. You can of course buy a secondhand machine, or use one passed down from a relative (note the vintage beauty shown opposite). It will probably be great, just get it serviced before you begin sewing to make sure it is in top condition. Either contact your local sewing center or google "sewing machine service" in your area and a plethora of companies will pop up. Many of these companies are mobile, so will come to you.

Sewing machines come with a starter selection of accessories including your basic sewing feet, needles, and bobbins. It's worth making sure you have a walking foot and a selection of sewing machine needles for leather. You could also invest in a quilting foot if you plan to machine-quilt. You can buy everything online or through a store.

If sewing on a machine is new to you, find a local class in which they show you the rudiments. It's a great investment of your time and money—but make sure you go to a class in which you can take your own machine.

Needles and Pins

There is an extraordinary array of needles and pins to be found. Here are the essentials:

Hand-Stitching Needles

- *Sharps*—These are your general-purpose needles. Each pack will have a variety of sizes to use with different weights of fabric.
- *Quilters/betweens*—For hand-quilting. They have a rounded end that makes them more comfortable to use.
- *Embroidery/crewel*—For embroidery or thicker threads.
- *Darning/tapestry needles*—For working with wool.

Pins

- *Dressmaker's pins*—Extra-fine and easy to use.
- *Quilting/glass-headed pins*—Longer, for working through layers of fabric.
- *Entomology pins*—For very fine fabrics.

Cutting

- *Dressmaker's scissors*—Make sure they are sharp and of good quality. And never be tempted to use them for cutting paper.
- *Household scissors*—For the cutting of said paper and patterns.
- *Thread scissors*—Tiny and useful. I generally have them on a ribbon around my neck as they disappear easily.
- *Pinking shears*—For zigzag edges that ravel less than straight edges, or to finish seams.
- *Utility knife*—Useful for cutting soft leather or small items.
- *Rotary cutter*—A rotary cutter is, in fact, a circular razor blade so needs to be treated with respect. You simply use it to cut fabric on a cutting mat. Use it to cut fabric for quilts, as it makes the job very fast.

Other Notions

- *Cutting mat*—A cutting mat provides a grid for you to line up your fabric. Used mostly for quilt making, it would be useful for many other projects. You can buy cutting mats in many sizes and with imperial or metric measurements. A mat 20in. × 13in. would be the smallest useful size for making quilts.
- *Quilter's ruler*—Made from transparent acrylic, they are designed to be used with cutters and mats and they make it easy to cut fabric accurately.
- *Seam ripper*—For rectifying mistakes. Make sure the blade is sharp.
- *Tailor's chalk or erasable pencils*—For tracing patterns and transferring markings.
- *Tailor's tape measure*—For measuring and slinging around your neck to look professional.
- *Long metal ruler*—For measuring long and straight lines.
- *Thimbles*—For hand-stitching. There are several types, made of metal or leather. Again, this will be complete personal preference, but I use a leather one as I find it more flexible and comfortable.
- *Masking tape*—From a D.I.Y. store—it is useful for marking quilting lines and keeping fabric straight.
- *Awl (bradawl)*—You'll find this in your toolbox. It is very useful for making holes. You can buy this in a hardware or haberdashery store.
- *Leather punch*—These will make different-sized holes and are very useful for straps, bags, and purses.
- *Lightweight hammer*—Again, raid the toolbox.
- *Iron*—With a steam option for perfectly pressed seams.
- *For dyeing*—Thick rubber gloves, plastic buckets, and rubber bands.
- *For upholstery*—Pliers, staple gun or upholstery tacks, wire wool, fine sandpaper, and methylated spirits.

Natural Dye

Dyeing can be a little messy, but the colors you can achieve by mixing natural cloth with colors from Mother Nature are well worth it.

Natural dyeing is simply the process in which yarn or fabric is immersed in a solution produced by boiling up selected raw materials, or dyestuffs. These may be from an animal, vegetable, or mineral source.

Natural dyes are a renewable resource—almost every plant in the world will give a fantastic color and they are literally on your doorstep. If they're not free, they can be created inexpensively or are the waste product of cooking or gardening. Dyeing with natural dyes has obvious ecological advantages—no chemicals, no nastiness. But they also create colors that are just magical, so I think the combination is a win-win on both practicality and aesthetics.

There are many books and courses that offer an in-depth education in the art of dyeing. For *Cloth*, I thought we'd keep it simple—a starting point to something that can become very addictive, very quickly.

There are two types of natural dyes. Substantive dyes are those that give a fast, lasting color without the need for extra chemical processes (or mordants) to fix the colors. Adjective dyes require the yarn or fabric to be treated with a mordant to make it more absorbent and allow the dye to bite and take hold. Different dyes use different mordants, but most mordants are mineral based—such as alum, tin, chrome, or iron. However, the oldest is urine—not very lovely to think about, but very effective.

Most dyes fall into the second category. If you don't mind the color being lighter or fading over time (and possibly bleeding) then you can skip the mordant when heating your water for dyeing. A simple mordant to use on all natural cloth is alum—readily available in a salt form. The simplest option is probably common table salt.

To dye fabric you need to bring water and your choice of dye to a boil, reduce to a simmer, and then add the mordant. After concocting the mixture, add the fabric and then let it soak in the dye. The longer the soak, the more intense the color.

Once you have the color you're aiming for, remove the fabric and rinse it in lukewarm water until the water runs clear. Then hand wash it with a gentle detergent.

The final color will vary depending on whether you use fresh or dried dyes, whether the water is hot or cold, what fabric you use, the type of mordant, and the pH level of the water. In addition, every natural cloth will take dye differently, as some fabrics are protein based and some plant based. This sounds very complicated but it isn't. I like a slight sense of "winging it" when I dye, but you can always use scraps of cloth to test color.

Dyestuffs

On this page is a list of plants, berries, bark, leaves, and powders that are perfect for dyeing. Have a rummage in your pantry or wander through your garden and neighborhood to find the perfect color. Powdered dyes are listed in the resources section (see page 185).

Useful equipment for dyeing

- Metal pots or pans (only to be used for dyeing)
- Tongs
- Stirrers or sticks
- Insulated rubber gloves—from a craft supply store
- A couple of buckets or plastic containers
- Pegs, clips, and rubber bands
- Glass jars for mordants to keep them safe
- An apron or a selection of old clothes
- Alum salts
- Your choice of dyestuff

Red/Pink

Bamboo—turkey red
Blackberries—dark red
Beetroot peelings—red
Cherries—dark pink
Crabapple bark—red/yellow
Elderberry—red
Grape skins—bright fuchsia
Madder root—red
Purple sage—red
Raspberries—red
Rosehips—pink
Roses and lavender—with a little mint and some lemon juice to activate the alkaloids, this makes a brilliant pink dye
Strawberries—pink

Purple/Blue

Basil—purplish gray
Blackberries—strong purple
Blueberries—purple
Cornflower petals—with alum, it gives blue
Elderberries—lavender
Grapes—purple
Hyacinth flowers—blue
Logwood—with alum, it gives purple to blue-purple
Mulberries—royal purple
Olives that have dropped from a tree—deep blue/purple
Ornamental plum tree leaves—purple gray
Red cabbage—mauve/purple
Saffron petals—blue/green

Green

Artichokes—green
Black-Eyed Susan flowers—bright olive/apple green
Hydrangea flowers—with added copper, a beautiful celery green
Broom stem—green
Calendula flowers—luminescent green
Camellia (pink, red petals)—green
Carrot tops—light green
Chamomile leaves—green
Grape leaves—shades of yellows to earthy chartreuse and deep greens
Grass—yellow green
Lilac flowers—green
Nettle—light yellow/green
Peppermint—dark khaki green
Red onion skin—lighter than forest green
Rosemary leaves—pale green
Snapdragon flowers—green
Sorrel roots—dark green
Spinach leaves—green

Black/Brown

Acorns (boiled)—light yellow/brown
Beluga black lentils (soaked in water overnight)—milk chocolate brown to a light brown when watered down
Birch bark (with alum)—light brown/buff
Broom bark—yellow/brown
Coffee grounds—dark brown
Dandelion roots—brown
Fennel flowers or leaves—yellow/brown
Iris roots—mid brown
Ivy twigs—yellow/brown
Juniper berries—brown
Oak bark—tan or oak color
Sumac leaves—black
Tea bags—light brown/tan
Walnut hulls—deep brown
Walnut husks—deep brown-black
Wild plum root—reddish/rusty brown

Yellow

Alfalfa seeds—yellow
Bay leaves—yellow
Brown onion skins—yellow
Celery leaves—pale yellow
Crocus—yellow
Daffodil flower heads (after they have died)—yellow
Dahlia flowers (red, yellow, orange flowers)—orange/yellow
Dandelion flowers—pale yellow
Heather plant—yellow
Marigold blossoms—yellow
Mimosa flowers—yellow
Paprika—pale yellow/light orange
Peach leaves—yellow
Poppy roots—earthy yellow
Sunflowers—yellow
Turmeric—bright yellow
Weld—bright yellow

FICTION 19

White gold— this is how history refers to cotton.

Of all the cloths in the world, cotton is the behemoth. Traded on the stock exchange, cotton is still the world's most important nonfood agricultural commodity. No other fiber has created such wealth or, conversely, such damage to countries and people. It's used everywhere, for many items—clothing, bedding, medical supplies, and food. Just look around your home and in your wardrobe to see the impact cotton has on an ordinary household. It is also a relatively "cheap" crop, which means cheap fabric: Probably why over 40 percent of the world's textiles are made from cotton.

Cotton is a renewable resource, but only if the resources are managed responsibly. Unfortunately, the sustainability of cotton growing and farmers' livelihoods can be threatened by poor crop protection, water abuse, diminished soil fertility, and—terribly—child and forced labor.

As a fiber cotton is so important and, although it has had its ups and downs over the last few hundred years, it is hoped that everything is improving: better-quality cotton and, more importantly, healthier land and people.

Cotton is a soft, fluffy staple fiber that grows in a "boll" on the plant's stem. The boll is a protective capsule that wraps itself around the seeds of the cotton plant to help them disperse in the wind. For the gardeners among you, the cotton plant is naturally perennial, which means that it lasts for more than one growing season. However, it is harnessed and treated as an annual, meaning that it goes from seed to harvest in one year. This ensures that the plants do not grow too large, are uniform in size, and produce their fiber at the same time.

Cotton is a member of the mallow family, which includes other plants such as marsh mallow, hollyhock, and hibiscus. Although there are 30 recognized species of cotton, only four are cultivated commercially— *Gossypium barbadense* (Egyptian and Sea Island cotton), *Gossypium hirsutum* (upland cotton), *Gossypium arboreum* (tree cotton), and *Gossypium herbaceum* (Levant cotton).

Although you have probably only seen images of puffy white cotton fields, cotton often grows in lovely shades of brown, pink, and green. These are usually grown as a specialty fiber and kept far, far away from white cotton to prevent color contamination. These natural-colored cottons are now being used by both boutique and large clothing companies as a naturally colored alternative to bleached or dyed white cotton.

Cotton is nonallergenic (which means it has no adverse reactions on your skin), breathable, and incredibly soft. It is very adaptable and can be blended with most other fibers. It has a very high absorbency rate and can hold up to 27 times its own weight in water. Cotton is also stronger when wet and keeps you warm in winter and cool in summer. It takes dye and any form of printing well. As a natural fiber it is probably the most useful, versatile, and cost-effective one there is. It is also our fabric of choice in clothing and homewares. Like all fabrics, there is high- and low-quality cotton available to choose from, but the variance is far greater. Sheets are known by their thread count (the number of threads per square inch or centimeter) and T-shirts by the quality of the raw cotton.

The plant is a shrub native to tropical and subtropical regions around the world, including the Americas, Africa, and India. Because of its tropical origins it needs warmth and sunshine for about half of the year, plus lots and lots of water. It takes an average of 2,250 gallons of water to grow 2.2lb of cotton lint—in other words, enough to make only one pair of jeans. As water resources become scarcer around the world, many countries that rely on cotton face financial difficulties and conflict, as well as potential environmental problems.

History

Cotton has been spun, woven, and dyed since prehistoric times. It clothed the people of ancient India, Egypt, and China before becoming the predominant textile of most modern nations, such as the United States and Britain. It seems to have spread seamlessly, without the romance of silk or the artisan culture of wool.

No one knows exactly how old this textile is but it seems to have always been there and always used—never as a premium cloth but in a very good support role. Archaeologists have found scraps of cotton bolls and pieces of cloth that are at least 7,000 years old in a Mexican cave. Cloth fragments in Pakistan dating from around 3,000 BC have also been uncovered. Around the same time, natives of the Egyptian Nile valley were making and wearing cotton clothing, and Egypt is still a significant producer.

Between 2,000 BC and 1,000 BC, cotton production was sweeping through India. From there, it spread to the Mediterranean and beyond, with Arab merchants bringing cotton to Europe around AD 800. During the late medieval period cotton was an imported fiber in northern Europe, without any knowledge of its origins, other than that it was a plant that produced a fiber. When Columbus discovered America in 1492 he found cotton already growing in the Bahamas and, by the end of the 16th century, cotton was grown and processed throughout the warmer regions of Asia and the Americas.

At the height of the British Empire it was against the law to either import or manufacture cloth from cotton from any country but Britain—just as in the wool industry. These harsh measures were to prevent the colonies creating large-scale production that would take away Britain's power. Americans, being ever resourceful, just planted their own seeds, and the U.S.A. is still one of the biggest growers and exporters of cotton today.

Up until the end of the 18th century, harvesting cotton was still done by hand (and, in some parts of the world, still is). But in 1793 the "gin," short for engine, was designed. It could pick ten times faster than by hand, which meant more cotton production.

When the Industrial Revolution arrived, cotton became Britain's biggest export. Manchester, or "Cottonopolis" to those in the know, was the center of the cotton industry, not just for Britain, but for the world. These mills were critical to the area's towns and villages but, like other methods of textile production in Britain, have all but disappeared. As the British expanded into India, so India's cotton production declined. British-imposed law forced India to supply only raw cotton, which they then had to buy back as manufactured textiles.

As India's productivity declined, that of the U.S.A. increased. Regrettably, cultivating and harvesting cotton became the leading occupation of African-American slaves. Even after emancipation, cotton remained a vital crop to the southern states. Newly freed black farmers and landless white farmers worked on white-owned cotton plantations in return for a share of the profits. But, as picking became mechanized, this manual labor disappeared as well.

Today around 25 million tons of cotton are produced worldwide every year. The largest producers are China and India, although the U.S.A. is the biggest exporter. There are around 25,000 cotton growers in the U.S.A. and approximately 180,000 small cotton farmers in Africa. Cotton production continues to grow and grow. Thankfully, organic and sustainable cotton production is growing the fastest of all—for more on the Organic Movement, see pages 88–89.

Production

Most cotton grown in the U.S.A., Europe, and Australia is harvested with mechanical equipment, but it is still hand-picked in developing countries.

After the cotton is picked, it is sent to a mill where it is fed into cleaning machines. These mix the cotton up and break it into smaller pieces, as well as removing any detritus. The cotton is then beaten to knock out the dirt and to separate it into even smaller pieces. The fibers are fed through a carding machine, in which they are separated into short and long fibers, with the short fibers being removed. From here, the process moves on to spinning, by which the cotton is reduced, straightened, and twisted. After all this mechanical torture, the cotton is ready to be made into cloth.

Once it is woven, it goes through a variety of processes before it becomes a finished fabric—boiling, burning, and bleaching to name a few. The processes used depend on the end product required. If needed, it is then dyed or printed—or both.

Cotton can be woven into cloth in three different ways. A plain weave will produce simple fabrics such as broadcloth, as well as mid-weight fabrics such as chambray; twill weaves make denim and khaki; and a satin weave is used for other fabrics such as sateen.

This process can be entirely mechanized, completely performed by hand, or somewhere in between. Thus, a hand-printed and hand-loomed cotton should be more expensive than commercially produced cottons, shouldn't it? Sadly, it often isn't.

Uses

I don't think there are very many things that cotton can't be used for. Sixty percent of it is turned into clothing (including our beloved jeans) and the rest is made into upholstery cloth, bedding and bathware, and yarn, as well as supplies for the medical industry. Cotton is also manufactured into tents, fishing nets, and bookbinding material. It was once used for fire hoses—I wonder how effective they were?

The fiber from one 500lb bale of cotton can produce 215 pairs of jeans, 3,000 diapers, or 680,000 cotton balls. Fabric can also be made from recycled cotton that otherwise would be thrown away during the spinning, weaving, or cutting process.

Almost all of the cotton plant can be turned into something useful—which is great. Leftover cottonseed is used to make cholesterol-free oil for cooking and as a high-energy feed for livestock. The oil can also be made into margarine, cosmetics, rubber, and candles, to name a few uses.

The short cotton fibers left from carding are called linters. They are used to make archival paper and dollar bills as well as cotton swabs and balls.

Fairtrade

It's obvious that cotton is an enormously important cloth. However, it is one that currently keeps the economic scales unbalanced. Developing countries, such as the African nations, cannot compete with their developed neighbors on price or productivity, which can then cause immense hardship. Some countries, such as Lithuania, are still criticized for employing child labor and damaging workers' health by exposure to intensive pesticides. However, it is now easy to find Fairtrade cotton as fabric, yarn, or a finished product—and it usually just feels better in every sense.

Cotton is our workaday, everyday cloth and is part of our daily lives. You will be wearing it, sleeping under it, and making lovely things from it. Cotton is good; it's just that some cottons are better.

Canvas Market Tote

Robust, useful, and delightful to look at—you can't ask much more from a tote. This bag is the perfect size for a farmers' market excursion, a day out, or even a night away.

By pairing sturdy artist's canvas with high-quality bridle-leather handles, you can make a bag that's not only practical for everyday use but also looks stylish and modern.

Finished Size

- 17½in. × 13½in. × 4½in.
- Seam allowances are ⅜in. and are included in the pattern pieces

Materials

- Tote outer and pocket—27½in. sturdy ivory cotton canvas—canvas is usually 47–57in. wide.
- Tote inner—19½in. lightweight cotton
- One leather handle kit (see resources on page 185)
- 100 percent cotton thread in a neutral color

Other Tools

- Tailor's chalk or dressmaker's pencil
- Fabric scissors
- Pins
- Sewing machine
- To attach the leather handles: awl, lightweight hammer, and towel or blanket

Cut

Cut out or trace the tote outer, tote inner, and pocket pattern pieces provided at the back of the book. ▣ Fold your tote outer fabric in half, right sides facing, and pin the pattern piece to it. Cut around the pattern, so that you cut out two outer pieces. ▣ Unfold the remaining fabric for the outer and pin the pocket pattern piece to it. Cut out one pocket.

▣ Fold your tote inner fabric in half, right sides facing, and pin the pattern piece to it. Cut around the pattern, so that you cut out two inner pieces.

Sew the Tote Outer

Join the tote outers right sides together, matching all the edges, and pin in place. ▣ Sew a ⅜in. seam down both sides and across the bottom of the pieces, making sure you backstitch at each end. Press the seams and keep your tote outer wrong side out. ▣ Next you need to create a flat bottom for your bag. With right sides together, match the bottom seam and one side seam to form a triangle in the bottom corner. Pin in place. Repeat this with the bottom seam and second side seam. You now have two triangles. ▣ Mark a line at right angles to the side seam at the point where the corner is 4½in. wide. Sew along this marked line and then repeat for the second bottom corner. This creates the bottom of your bag. Press both triangles to the bottom of the bag and hand-stitch in place.

Sew the Pocket

Turn in ⅜in. on both side edges of the pocket and press. ▣ Turn up ⅜in. on the bottom edge of the pocket over the sides and press. ▣ On the top edge, fold over ⅜in. and press. Then fold over ¾in. and press. Topstitch your top edge. ▣ Using the pattern piece as a placement guide, pin the pocket to one of the tote inner pieces with WS of pocket facing RS of tote inner. ▣ Sew together, close to the edges of the pocket piece leaving the top side unsewn. Reinforce the corners by sewing a small triangle on each of the top edge corners of the pocket.

Sew the Tote Inner

Repeat all the steps for the tote outer, but leave an 8in. opening centered along the bottom seam.

Finish the Tote

With the tote inner wrong side out and the tote outer right side out, slip the inner over the outer. The outer is taller than the inner so you will need to scrunch it down a little. Pin the raw top edges together making sure the side seams are aligned. Sew a ⅜in. seam all around the edge. Press the seams open. ▫ Turn the tote right side out through the tote inner's bottom opening. Push the inner back inside the outer. The top edge of the outer will fold inside the bag, giving you a sturdier top to attach your handles to. Press the bag all around the top edges and seams. Hand- or machine-stitch the tote inner's bottom edge closed.

Attach the Handles

From your pattern, mark the points on your bag where the handles will be positioned. Leather handle kits have their own attachment instructions so follow these using the tools outlined on page 27.

Your market tote is complete.

Design Thoughts

If ivory is not your color or canvas doesn't excite you, there are many other fabrics that you could use for this tote. Waxed canvas would be super stylish (and very practical), as would a lovely Japanese denim. Sturdy wool tartans would be practical and any form of upholstery fabric would also work. Your lining could also be a good place to add some color or pattern. A soft stripe or an Indian block print would be great, as would some vintage floral bark cloth. Perhaps a waterproof lining might be more practical.

If you don't want to use leather handles, you can replace these with sturdy cotton webbing. Simply measure the length you would like—shoulder or carry-bag length—and add 4in. to each of the two handles to create your cutting length. When you position the handles, turn under 2in. on each end, pin, and sew in place, making sure you sew enough to firmly attach the handles.

Simple Cotton Quilt

Quilts can be both complicated and time consuming both in the design process and in the actual making. Many people would love to make them, yet they feel overwhelmed by the process. But it doesn't have to be complicated, and I believe that making should never be anything but enjoyable. Some of my favorite historical quilts are so simple—just one or two beautiful fabrics. The magic comes from the hand of the maker—how they put the fabrics together and how they stitch them. We all have a different approach to needle and thread. Some of us need every stitch to be precise, others are more *wabi sabi* in their approach. Both are fine—that's the great thing about quilts, they are a complete reflection of who you are, which is wonderful.

So this quilt is just simple squares and two fabrics—albeit two very beautiful fabrics. It's also held together with a simple running stitch and is a really useful size. As an entry into quilt making, it's the ideal project.

Finished Size

- 63in. × 63in. (but you can increase or reduce the size by 3¼in. increments)
- Seam allowances are ⅜in. and are included in the cutting sizes.

Materials

- Invest in special cloth for this quilt. For the piece shown opposite, I used my favorite plain Indian kantha cotton and paired it with a Japanese indigo-dyed cotton. It looks like regular dotty cloth until you get up close and then you can see the beautiful handiwork of the irregular spots. For my backing, I've used a wonderful African wax print—both for color and a little melding together of cultures.
- 98in. plain cotton of choice—width at least 43½in.
- 78in. printed cotton of choice—width at least 43½in.
- 157in. cotton, for the backing—width at least 43½in.
- 100 percent cotton thread in a neutral color
- 100 percent cotton quilting thread in your chosen color
- A piece of cotton batting 67in. × 67in.

Other Tools

- Iron and ironing board
- Fabric scissors
- Ruler
- Tailor's chalk or dressmaker's pencil
- Rotary cutter
- Cutting mat
- Pins
- Sewing machine
- Masking tape
- Quilting needle

Prepare

Prewash the fabric on a warm wash to eliminate any shrinkage or dye run. Dry, then press with a hot iron.

Cut

Cut away the selvage from both edges of your two fabrics. ▢ Using a rotary cutter and cutting mat, cut twenty 4in. strips from your plain fabric. Cut each of these strips into 4in. squares, discarding any scraps. Cut the remaining plain fabric into 2in. strips. These will be used for the quilt binding. ▢ Cut twenty 4in. strips from your patterned fabric. Cut each of these strips into 4in. squares.

Sew the Quilt Top

You need to sew twenty rows of twenty squares, alternating plain and patterned fabrics. ▢ Start by pinning one plain and one patterned square right sides together and sewing along one edge. Use a ⅜in. seam allowance. If you don't have this marked on your sewing machine, simply measure ⅜in. from your needle and mark with a permanent marker or a piece of scotch tape. Continue to add squares until you have one row of twenty squares. Snip away any threads and press all the seams open. ▢ Repeat this for nineteen more rows, making sure that each row is pressed with the seams open. ▢ Join the first two rows together, pinning at the seam lines. Make sure that you have alternate squares—that is, a plain piece pinned to a patterned piece. Each odd row, i.e. 1, 3, 5, will start with a plain piece and finish with a patterned piece. Each even row will begin with a patterned and finish with a plain piece. This is how you create the "checkerboard" look of the quilt. Sew the two rows together, making sure that all the seams match. Press the seam lines open. ▢ Join the remaining eighteen rows together. You now have a finished quilt top. ▢ Now make your quilt backing. You may have one piece of fabric large enough for your backing, or you may need to sew several pieces together. Sew your choice of fabrics together, right sides facing, with a ⅜in. seam allowance, until you have a square at least 67in. × 67in., or 4in. larger than your quilt top if you have adjusted the size.

Build the Quilt

Press your backing and lay it right side down, preferably on a hard and clean surface. A floor would be perfect. Smooth out the backing carefully so that there are no creases and then using long pieces of masking tape, tape the quilt down at points all the way around the sides (but not the corners as this stretches the quilt), smoothing as you go. This holds the backing flat, taut, and square. ▢ Lay your batting on top, smoothing it out, matching it to the backing. If your batting is bigger than your backing, trim it down to match. ▢ Press your quilt top until it's perfect, doing a final check for any loose threads as you go. ▢ Lay the quilt top on the batting right side up, making sure it is square with the backing. You now need to hold the three layers together so that you can quilt. Use long, fine pins and, starting from either the center or one side of the quilt, pin across the whole quilt every 4–6in., smoothing as you go. Alternatively you can run long basting stitches across the whole quilt—again in 4–6in. rows.

Finishing your Quilt

To finish and bind your quilt, follow the instructions for the Kimono Silk Quilt on page 104.

Well done—your quilt is finished!

Design Thoughts

You can make this quilt bigger or smaller—teeny for a doll's quilt or super large for a king-sized bed. You can most certainly use more than two fabrics—try using one plain and as many patterned fabrics as you like. You could be random in your placement of these, or create an order so that there is repetition in the quilt.

You can use another fabric for the binding to add contrast, or scraps to create the backing rather than a single piece of cloth.

Denim Apron

When I lived in New Zealand, I owned a homewares store for many years. We designed and manufactured all of the textile goods—from quilts, pillows, and pajamas to one of my favorites, our Japanese denim aprons. I'd always found aprons to be too short or frilly to be useful or aesthetically pleasing. I wanted to create something robust enough to deal with my cooking style (messy) but still stylish and, of course, practical. So, taking inspiration from my favorite pair of jeans, I sourced some great dark Japanese denim and designed a simple, long apron. It has pockets for hands and tea-towels, a loop for tongs or spoons and flexible ties so that anyone can wear it. It can also be washed and washed, which means, as aprons go, it's completely in the spirit of William Morris's much-lauded ethos—it is useful as well as very good-looking.

To update it slightly, I've added an extra pocket for your cell phone, something not so vital back then. . .

Finished Size

- 34½in. (w) × 41½in. (h)
- Seam allowances are ⅜in. and are included in the pattern pieces.

Materials

- 45in. dark cotton denim. Denim usually comes in wide widths, so you will have some wastage. You could use the leftovers for many of the other projects in *Cloth*. Although I have used a Japanese denim, if you find this hard to source, any denim is fine.
- 100 percent cotton thread in a dark blue to match your denim
- 100 percent cotton thread in white/ivory to match your cotton tape color
- 138in. natural colored cotton tape
- ⅜in. eyelet kit (⅜in. refers to the inside hole measurement). You will use 4 of the ten eyelets included and the tools you need to apply the eyelets to the apron. You can find these online or in good haberdashery stores.

Other Tools

- Iron and ironing board
- Pins
- Tailor's chalk or dressmaker's pencil
- Fabric scissors
- Sewing machine

Prepare

Prewash the fabric on a warm wash to eliminate any shrinkage or dye run, as dark denim can "rub" off excess color. Dry, then press with a hot iron. Cut out or trace the apron pattern pieces provided in the back of the book—the apron body and two pockets.

Cut

Using weights or pins, secure the pattern pieces to the denim, making sure that the pieces run down the grain of the fabric, not at angles to it. Trace around each pattern piece, making sure you transfer pocket and eyelet position markings from the patterns to the fabric. Cut out the apron body and two pockets.

Thread your machine with the dark blue thread. ⊡ On the top and bottom edge of the apron, fold over ³⁄₈in. toward the wrong side and press with a hot iron. Turn over another ³⁄₈in. toward the wrong side and press again. Pin and stitch this down, sewing close to the edge and to the end. ⊡ Repeat this for the two side seams. Now repeat for the two curved seams, being careful not to stretch the seams as you go. If you have particularly sturdy denim, you may want to clip the fabric so that you are able to fold on the curve. The main body of your apron is complete. ⊡ Take the large pocket piece and fold the top edge over ³⁄₈in. toward the wrong side. Fold over and press another ³⁄₈in. toward the wrong side. Pin and stitch this down, sewing close to the edge. ⊡ Fold over ³⁄₈in. on the bottom edge of the large pocket piece and press. Repeat with the two side seams. ⊡ Cut a 6in. piece of the cotton tape and fold in half crosswise. Pin this to the wrong side of the top lefthand side of the pocket, making sure the folded end is left free, so that you create a loop.

Pin the pocket to the main body of the apron, matching up the points from the pattern. Sew the pocket to the main body around the sides and bottom, ¹⁄₄in. from the edge, backstitching at the top corners and making sure you catch the cotton tape in the stitching. ⊡ Change to the white or ivory thread. If you haven't already, transfer the extra pocket seam line from the pattern to the pocket using chalk or a pencil. Topstitch down the center line of your pocket as marked on your pattern, backstitching at the top edge for robustness. Then topstitch over the seam line where the cotton tape is positioned. ⊡ Take the small pocket piece and fold the top edge over ³⁄₈in. toward the wrong side. Press and fold over another ³⁄₈in. toward the wrong side. Pin and stitch this down, sewing close to the edge. ⊡ Change back to your dark blue thread. Fold over ³⁄₈in. on the bottom edge and press, and repeat with the two side seams. Pin the pocket to the main body of the apron, matching up the points from the pattern. Sew the pocket to the main body around the sides and bottom edges of the pocket, using a ¹⁄₄in. seam allowance and backstitching at the top corners.

Mark the eyelet positions on your apron—two at the top and one on each side. Insert the eyelets following the instructions on the kit. As you only need four sets of eyelets, you might want to practice with a spare pair of eyelets to avoid any mistakes—especially since you are so close to finishing. ⊡ Once you have inserted the eyelets you only need to attach the cotton tape to finish your aprons. Cut the remaining tape into two 39in. lengths and two 24in. lengths. Knot the two short lengths into the eyelets at the top of your apron and the two long lengths into the eyelets at the sides of your apron. Put the apron on and tie the neck tape into a bow, making sure it sits in a comfortable position. You can trim any excess neck tape away.

That's it—your denim apron is complete.

Design Thoughts

I've added an extra design detail by using two different thread colors. You don't have to do this. You could use all dark blue, or all ivory—or actually any color of your choice. Red thread looks particularly good with dark denim. Choose a different denim finish if you fancy, or one with a little bit of stretch in it—this makes the frantic movements of cooking a little easier.

We also made these aprons in hemp, which look and feel fantastic. Any sturdy linen or hemp would be wonderful—vintage or new.

You add interest with your cotton tape and eyelets. I've used nickel eyelets but you can use brass or even copper. Cotton tapes are available in different widths and strengths. They also come in stripes and different colors—and you can get linen tape as well.

If you are particularly tall or short, measure the pattern piece against you and add or subtract length as required—the apron is meant to sit at the mid-shin point but you can adjust upward, if required.

Liberty Print Pillow

When I look at Liberty Tana Lawn, I think of Arthur Liberty and his incredibly intuitive and creative vision. I think of a store that was, and still is, like no other. With shop assistants wafting around in kimonos and the fabulous pre-Raphaelite set roaming its floors, the famous store was at the cutting edge of interiors. Fast-forward 140 years and, though it might not be at the height of the current zeitgeist, Liberty fabrics will always be intrinsically cool. There will always be a print or colorway that draws you back in, whether for your home, yourself, or your children. Liberty's global take on the design of its fabrics means that Tana Lawn will sit as comfortably with Arts and Crafts furniture as it does with Bauhaus.

Using pillows is a thoughtful way to introduce Liberty prints into your home. Tana Lawn is wider than most cottons (54in.) so you can make a proper 20in. pillow from just over half a yard. You can make one pillow or buy several different prints and mix and match as I've done. They are quick to make and are also perfect as birthday or housewarming presents.

Finished Size

- 20in. × 20in.
- Seam allowances are ⅜in. and are included in the cutting sizes.

Materials

- 21½in. Liberty Tana lawn per pillow
- 100 percent cotton thread in a neutral or contrasting color

Other Tools

- Iron and ironing board
- Long ruler—at least 24in. long
- Tailor's chalk or dressmaker's pencil
- Fabric scissors
- Pins
- Sewing machine
- 20in. feather and down pillow form per pillow

Prepare

Prewash the fabric on a warm wash to eliminate any shrinkage. Dry, then press with a hot iron.

Cut

Trim each length of fabric down to 20½in. and trim away the selvage. (Sometimes, when fabric is cut in a store, they may not cut it perfectly straight, so it's best to buy a little bit more to be safe.) From the trimmed length, cut one 20½in. square. This will be your pillow front. Fold the remaining fabric in half and press. Cut along the pressed point. You should have two pieces approx. 20½in. × 16½in. These together will be your pillow back.

Plan

If you are sewing just one pillow, you don't need to worry about planning. If, however, you are making more than one pillow and are going to mix fabrics, this is the time to plan which fronts will go with which backs. You can have one, two, or three fabrics per pillow.

Sew the Pillow Backs

On the long edge of one back piece, turn over ³⁄₈in. to the wrong side and press. Turn over again by ³⁄₄in., press, and pin in place. ▢ Topstitch this in either one or two rows, depending on the look you like. ▢ Repeat this for the other pillow back piece.

Sew the Pillow

Place the pillow front right side up. Take one pillow back piece and place it, right side down, on top of the pillow front, with the raw edges matching. The topstitched edge should be towards the center. ▢ Place the second pillow back piece, right side down, on top with the raw edges matching those on the front sides. ▢ The two topstitched edges of the back pieces should overlap. This is called an envelope closure. ▢ Pin the top and two backs together, making sure you pin through all three layers when necessary. ▢ Sew ³⁄₈in. in from the edge around all four edges. ▢ Press the seams open and trim the corners. ▢ Turn the pillow right sides out and gently push out the corners to make them sharp. Press again.

Insert a pillow form, and your Liberty print pillow is complete.

Design Thoughts

Unlike sofas and chairs, new pillows can be created with a very modest budget. Once you have grasped the super-simple construction of a pillow with an envelope closure (super simple), you can whip up a batch of new covers in an hour or two. You can use almost any weight of fabric for a pillow—from silk to wool kilims.

You can use Liberty print just for the front and a plain or dramatically contrasting fabric for the back. Pick out a color from the print and mix it to tonally match a rough textured linen or a tactile cotton velvet.

Delve into quilt fabric stores (or online) for other quilting cotton prints from the likes of Kaffe Fassett, Amy Butler, or Lotta Jansdotter. These cottons are usually in bold prints and on-trend colorways if that's important, as well as being really cost effective.

Ethnic fabric stores are a great source of bold prints for very little expenditure. African Wax prints come in bolts of 4¹⁄₂–6yds—that's a lot of pillows for not a great deal of money! Similarly, Indian block prints and Cambodian silks both come in vibrant shades and patterns, which is perfect for a pillow. Japanese fabrics are usually more expensive, but are often worth it—the color palettes are usually subtle and the fabric is beautifully textured.

Waxed Cotton Purses

Waxed cotton is a wonderful fabric, both in visual appeal and versatility. It is simply cotton impregnated with a paraffin-based wax, which is then woven into a cloth. Created in the 1850s, it's waterproof yet breathable and was the sailing and military industries' cloth of choice until the 1960s. As modern, lighter, and cheaper fabrics such as nylon were introduced, waxed cotton was sadly put aside. However, it's safe to say that in recent years it has had a big resurgence in popularity. It's visually very attractive and incredibly practical. It mixes well with all other natural fibers, especially leather and canvas, and can look both functional and luxurious.

It's manufactured in great colors—black (obviously), gray, navy, Barbour olive, and various shades of tan. This beautiful fabric and the easy construction method make these purses a winning project.

Finished Size

These purses can be made in any size. Decide on what you would like to use them for and work out the width and length you need.

Materials

- A piece of waxed cotton fabric, suitable in size for your purse. It's easiest to buy online in half or full yard.
- A piece of lining cotton—the same size as your waxed cotton
- 100 percent cotton thread to match the waxed cotton
- Zipper—the same size as the cut size of your purse, or up to ¾in. longer. You can use metal- or plastic-toothed zippers for these purses.

Other Tools

- Long ruler—at least 24in. long
- Tailor's chalk or dressmaker's pencil
- Fabric scissors
- Pins
- Sewing machine with a zipper foot

Cut

Decide how large you want your purse to be and cut two pieces of waxed cotton and two pieces of lining cotton to this size, plus ¾in. extra in both length and width for the seam allowances.

Sew

Put the zipper foot on your sewing machine. Place your zipper face down on the right side of one of the waxed cotton pieces and pin it in place. Stitch together, close to the zipper coils. Place the lining fabric right sides together with the waxed cotton outer sandwiching the zipper. Pin into place. Stitch as you did with the waxed cotton—try to line up the two stitching lines. Press the seam and clip any loose threads. Turn the lining over the zipper and match the wrong side of the lining to the wrong side of the waxed cotton outer. Press each piece away from the zipper. Repeat for the second piece of waxed cotton and lining pieces. Press the seam and clip any loose threads. As an optional extra, on the right side of the waxed cotton piece, topstitch close to the zipper. Change back to a normal foot on your sewing machine.

Put the two waxed cotton pieces right sides together and stitch around the remaining three sides. Repeat for the lining but leave a gap in the bottom seam so that you can turn the purse through to the right side. Press the seams and clip the corners.

⊡ Turn the purse right side out through the gap in the lining and then slip-stitch the lining closed. Push the lining back inside the purse, and you're done.

Optional

To create a purse with a flat bottom, you need to match the bottom seam and one side seam to form a triangle in the bottom corner. Pin into place. Repeat this with the bottom seam and second side seam. You now have two triangles. Mark a line at right angles to the side seam, between $1\frac{1}{2}$ in. and 4 in., and sew across it. Repeat for the other corner and then repeat the process for the lining, making sure each set of triangles have the same measurements. Press the seams again and trim off the excess fabric from the corners.

Design Thoughts

Waxed cotton is not only incredibly stylish (in my humble opinion), but also totally fit for purpose for these purses as it is waterproof and wipeable. However, waxed cotton is only one type of fabric that you can use for these purses.

If you need a sturdy purse, then a strong cotton canvas or Japanese denim would be great. A fine wool felt would be lovely and also protective for sharp or breakable possessions. If you have leftover leather from other projects, then it would be wonderful to use here (just make sure you change to a leather needle on your sewing machine).

Any cotton fabric will work for the lining—patterned or plain, new or vintage. If you want to make a large zipper purse for your iPad, Kindle, or laptop make sure that the lining is thick or padded for protection—felt would be great.

Sometimes I reverse the order of the outer and the lining, i.e., put the heavyweight fabric on the inside and the pretty/patterned cotton on the outer. This is great for make-up purses or where anything sharp or potentially leaky may be stored.

To finish off your purse design, you can choose from a wide variety of zippers. Metal-toothed zippers are available in many colors with brass, copper, or nickel teeth in a variety of finishes. There are also chunky plastic and fine invisible zippers. Search at fairs or online for great vintage zippers for a different look again. You can buy dyeable zippers, so that you can make simple white cotton or linen purses that you then dip or tie-dye (very nice indeed).

Furoshiki

Oh, the furoshiki! A simple square of cloth that can be so many things. Handbag, bottle carrier, or gift wrapper—this ancient Japanese carrying device is still popular and relevant today. There are definitely times and places for lovely leather bags. But there should be room for one or three of these inside any bag. It's a very clever invention, in which the design and usefulness is based on a tying method. The core bag is simply a square of fabric in a color or pattern of your choice. Make one or ten—you'll use them everywhere and for many reasons.

Finished Size

- 29½in. × 29½in.
- Seam allowances are ¼in. and are included in the cutting sizes.

Materials

- A 30in. × 30in. square of cotton or light linen fabric to make each furoshiki. I've used some wonderful subtle block prints and khadi cotton from a Fairtrade collective in India. Although slightly more expensive than many cottons, it's worth the extra money as I know it's been block-printed by hand and, also, because I know that a family's livelihood is just a little richer through my purchase.
- Silk embroidery thread in a color of your choice

Other Tools

- Iron and ironing board
- Long ruler—at least 24in. long
- Tailor's chalk or dressmaker's pencil
- Fabric scissors
- Pins
- Embroidery needle

Prepare

Prewash the fabric on a warm wash to eliminate any shrinkage and dye runs. Dry, then press with a hot iron.

Cut

For each furoshiki, measure and mark out a 30in. square on the wrong side of the fabric. Then cut out.

Sew

Fold over each edge of the furoshiki ¼in. toward the center, on the wrong side of the fabric. Press with an iron. Fold over another ¼in. on all four edges and press again.
- Pin these folds down with the pins inserted horizontally to the edge (this will make hand-stitching easier). - Thread your embroidery needle and simply stitch a running stitch around all four sides. When you come back to the beginning, knot on the wrong side and snip the excess thread. - Your furoshiki square is complete. Now follow any of the lovely illustrations on page 49 to wrap it into shape.

Design Thoughts

You could easily empty your fabric cupboard making these. You need a black one for those serious moments, an African wax-print one for the weekend, as well as cheerful vintage prints for small hands to carry. Be contrasting with your embroidery thread or subtle, depending on your tastes and the end use. Use wool as a chunkier contrast or metallic thread for something a little more special. For once, don't change the size, but do change the fabric to suit your own aesthetic.

Hand Bag Wrap

Place your goods in the center of the furoshiki.

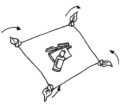

Tie a single knot at each corner, leaving a tail at the ends.

Tie two opposite corners together and repeat with the second two corners.

Book Wrap

Place your book in the center of the furoshiki.

Wrap one side over the book and tuck underneath. Repeat with the opposite side.

Your book will be covered. Pull up the two remaining corners as triangles.

Tie into a knot, leaving enough room to carry.

Flower Wrap

Place your bunch of flowers near the top and center of the wrap.

Fold back approx. 2in. of the furoshiki.

Bring these edges to the front and tie a knot.

Bring the bottom over the front of the flowers and turn over approx. 2in.

Wrap around the back and then to the front, tying a knot to secure.

Shoulder Bag Wrap

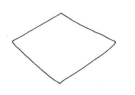

Lay the furoshiki flat.

Tie a knot on two diagonally opposite corners.

Turn the furoshiki around so that the knots are on the inside.

Twist the remaining two corners to form handles.

Tie into a knot, leaving enough room to carry on your shoulder.

Cotton Gauze Tent

This is just a little bit of magic. A hideaway, a resting place, a room within a room. As magical for adults as it is for children. We love small nooks, hiding-places in which we can see but not necessarily be seen. A place for pillows and books, music and chocolates. A solo place or a place to share stories and secrets. Cotton gauze has a wonderful shadowlike quality. You can see light and shapes but not hard reality—which is where the escapism begins.

There's no sewing involved (unless you want to), just some foraging, draping, and tying. The most difficult part will be finding the perfect spot in which to build your private space.

Finished Size

There is no defined size for these tents. You need to decide whether it's for small humans or grown-ups and whether you want to stand up or lay low.

Materials

- 11–22yds cotton gauze. You can usually buy this very easily and cheaply on rolls of this length.
- 9–12 sturdy coppiced lengths of hazel or other wood, or thick bamboo sticks. Decide on the height you would like the apex of the tent to be and get wood or bamboo approx. 24in. longer than this. Proper garden centers are the perfect source for these, or you can buy coppiced lengths online.
- Approx. 2 yards rope or thick string
- Felt scraps—if building your tent indoors

Other Tools

- Iron and ironing board (optional)
- Tape measure
- Fabric scissors
- Sewing machine (optional)

Prepare

Prewash your gauze on a warm wash to eliminate any shrinkage. Dry, then press with a hot iron if you want it to be smooth.

Make

With the wood or bamboo sticks lying in a bundle on the ground, tie them together with some of the rope or string, about 12–20in. from the top. Stand them up and spread the wood/sticks on the ground level to form an apex. If the tent is outside, you can tap each one into the ground to increase stability. If the tent is going to be inside, cut up some felt scraps to slip under the bottom ends of the sticks to prevent any damage to the floor surface. Roughly measure the height of your tent. Add 12in. to this measurement and cut widths of gauze to this length. You will need 4–6 drops to wrap around the whole tent. You can join the lengths together with vertical seams, or leave them as individual lengths. Tie the gauze securely around the top of the structure with the remaining rope, overlapping edges if needed. Set pillows, blankets, music, and books inside for a very pleasant way to spend a few hours.

Design Thoughts

Decorate your tent by painting or dyeing the gauze, or pinning vintage ribbons and garlands to it. Paint the wood or use colored rope. Change the gauze to a cotton sheet for a little more privacy (or if that's what you have to hand).

Whatever you do, keep this simple because, like wild camping or an unplanned picnic, the magic is in the ease and spontaneity.

Cotton Scrap Rag Rug

Humble and utilitarian, the history of rag rug making goes back hundreds of years. Before industrialization, every scrap of fabric was precious and nothing went to waste. Every item of worn-out clothing or bedding was carefully saved. Remnants were cut into strips, sewn together, and rolled into big balls to be made into rugs when time allowed. These rugs, although they were found mostly in homes of little wealth, had an undeniable beauty. And although they are time-consuming to make, the finished result will not only be worth it on a practical level, but could also show the story of years of your cloth-gathering.

Finished size

Any size you like

Materials

- Cotton fabric scraps or pieces of fabric. The amount you need depends on both the size of the rug and the thickness of the cloth. All the fabric needs to be a similar weight but you can use anything from old shirts and leftover quilting cloth to children's clothes. I have used a mixture of khadi cotton, Liberty prints, ticking and cotton scraps from other projects.
- Upholstery thread in a neutral color—make sure you match the tone of the fabric

Other Tools

- Ruler
- Tailor's chalk or dressmaker's pencil
- Rotary cutter and cutting mat
- Sewing machine
- Iron and ironing board
- Tapestry needle

Cut

Start by cuttting any items of clothing into flat pieces of cloth. Using a rotary cutter and cutting mat, cut all the fabric into 2in.-width strips, of any length. ▫ Trim your short ends to make sure that they are square. Create three piles of a roughly even size. You can group fabrics by color or be completely random in your choice.

Prepare

Take the first pile. Join all the strips into one by placing two short ends right sides together and then sewing a ³⁄₈in. seam. You can do this by either machine- or hand-stitching. ▫ The total strip length needed depends on the size of the rug you want to make; you'll need many more strips for larger rugs, but you can always add additional strips later if the rug isn't as big as you would like. This is an evolving project on which you can spend a few days or a whole summer. ▫ Fold the two long edges of each strip ¼in. toward the center, wrong sides together, and press with a warm iron. Fold the fabric strip in half lengthwise and press again. You'll end up with a ³⁄₄in.-wide folded strip with no raw edges showing. Roll this strip into a ball. ▫ Repeat for the remaining two piles. You now have three balls ready for braiding.

Make

Make a loose knot by joining one end from each of the three balls. Find a doorknob or hook that is a comfortable height to work from and slip the knot over it. ⊡ Start braiding the three strips using the normal three-strand method (like braiding your hair) until the braid is approx. 15–20in. long. ⊡ Then start to coil the braid into a spiral, starting at the knotted end. Place your coil on a flat surface. This will ensure that your rug lies flat with each coil. Using the tapestry needle and thread, stitch the coil together on the back of the rug, keeping the beginning knot on what will be the back of the rug. Braid another 20–40in. and then go back to coiling and stitching. Keep alternating between the two until you have reached the size of the rug you want, or you need to add more fabric. ⊡ When you get to the end of the rug, make sure you tuck and stitch the end of your braid so that the tail is on the bottom of your rug and will be hidden when you turn it over.

Snip any excess fabric from your center knot, and your rug is complete.

Design Thoughts

This is a project that you can and probably should create over time. It was originally created for using up scraps and because of this the rug may only grow as shirts wear out, children's dresses become too small, or fabric scraps become available. Don't rush it or plan it too much—it isn't quick, but then sometimes beauty is worth waiting for.

The Red Thread: A Little Love Story and A Useful List

An invisible red thread
Connects those who are
    destined to meet,
Regardless of time,
Place, or circumstance.
The thread may stretch
    and tangle
But never break.

CHINESE PROVERB

Chinese folklore uses the image of the red thread to describe destiny—that amid the unknown everything in life is predetermined. The notion of thread, and using thread, has always been used as a symbol of connection and love—stitching time—the threads that bind. The needle and thread are for making and mending but also for connecting and creating stories that stitch lives together.

There are only a few types of thread that you need, although there are a plethora available. I've not included man-made threads as I think they defeat the point of making with natural cloth. You can use polyester or mixed thread if you prefer.

Cotton machine-sewing thread is strong and wonderfully soft. It takes dye beautifully. Choose mercerized cotton for strength and a soft sheen. It comes in different thicknesses to work with different-weight cloths—the higher the number of the thread, the finer the fabric it should be used with.

Hand-quilting cotton is a super-strong waxed thread specifically for hand-quilting and hand-sewing. You can use it for quilting, bookbinding, paper, and leather. It is a stiffer thread, so will sew smoothly through heavier fabrics.

Pure silk thread—how lovely! It is perfect for hand- or machine-stitching on fine and delicate fabrics. Again, it is available in different thicknesses.

Linen thread is a strong and natural hand-sewing thread that is perfect for bags and leather goods.

Stranded embroidery thread comes in either silk or cotton. The strands can be separated if you want to use a finer thread for hand-stitching, or left as they are for lovely embellishment.

WOOL ⁵⁷

Kingdoms have been founded on it, fortunes made and lost because of it. Wool is the original cloth created and traded by man.

Of all the textiles in *Cloth*, wool is the most versatile, the most commercial, and the longest storyteller of people and their nations. Navajo Indians wrapped themselves in brightly colored woolen blankets and the gentlewomen of the 17th century found knitting to be a most suitable pastime. It has expertly clothed our war heroes (and villains) and ensured the ancient Greeks had comfortable and warm helmets. Our grandparents' suits were skillfully crafted from beautifully woven cloth, and it's a testament to the quality that they are usually in pristine condition today.

We can knit with it, felt it, fashion a fine cashmere sweater or a thick nubbly overcoat from it—we can even bury our toes in its deep pile. We swaddle our babies in it and our beds are wrapped in blankets made from it. Although feather comforters are very practical, it's not quite the same experience as being tucked in with a soft and heavy wool blanket. We can be kept warm or cool with it—think of the Bedouin and their woolen clothing, which helps them survive extraordinary desert temperatures. The weight and warmth of wool becomes both a physical and a psychological comfort. It is visual and tactile—the ultimate comfort cloth.

The wool industry created vital economies for towns, cities, and even countries, but it has waned from its historical peak. Farmers are switching from wool to meat farming to keep their flocks afloat. But there are glimmers of hope, with rare breeds being revitalized and small, specialized industries coming back to life. This is the work of a passionate few, so I think it's worth seeking out these artisans and makers and using their wool, which has resonance and provenance. Look at the resource section for a list of interesting people and businesses (see page 189).

Wool is shorn primarily from sheep as well as goats and llamas, so it is an animal fiber as opposed to plant-based fibers such as linen or cotton. It varies from super-fine merino fiber, similar to cashmere, to very coarse hairy wools such as Donegal tweed. It has the unique ability to stretch much farther than silk, cotton, or other natural fibers and regains its original shape after being stretched—so it molds perfectly to us or our furniture.

Wool can also be produced by other, more indulgent fibers, including cashmere and mohair from goats, qiviut from musk oxen, vicuña, alpaca and camel from animals in the camel family, and angora from rabbits. They may be less hardwearing than the fibers from our friend the sheep, but they are very special indeed.

Untreated wool can withstand temperatures of at least 1,060°F before it ignites—over twice that of cotton. As it burns it releases a foam that blocks access to oxygen, therefore smothering the flame—which is incredible. Also, it doesn't melt.

Wool garments are much less likely to spark or cling to the body, as wool resists static electricity. The use of wool car-seat covers or carpets reduces the risk of a shock to human hands. So, you can understand why firefighters wear wool and why wool carpets are specified for high-safety environments, such as trains and airplanes. (It also makes you wonder why there are man-made alternatives at all.)

Wool can absorb a third of its own weight in water before it starts to feel damp. And because it wicks water away from the skin, it helps keep your temperature even (remember the Bedouin and the summer-weight wool suits of our forefathers).

And last, but not least, wool is considered to be hypoallergenic by the medical profession, which means no irritation to the skin. *I like to think of it as wonderwool.*

History

Wool has existed since the domestication of sheep and goats more than 10,000 years ago and wool fabric was readily available to all echelons of society long before silk or cotton—fabrics that were considered luxuries and reserved for the upper classes. They say that sheep were the second domesticated animal after the prehistoric version of the dog. It would seem fortunate man didn't try the reverse order. . .

Prehistoric men clothed themselves in sheepskins and, by about 3,000 BC, Sumerian men were depicted in exceptionally stylish woven woolen skirts.

Woolly sheep were introduced into Europe from the Near East in 4,000 BC, and the oldest known European wool textile was made around 1,500 BC and discovered preserved in a Danish bog.

The Bible tells us of the white wool of Hebron, traded in the markets of Damascus, and we know that the Romans introduced sheep shearing. They—the Romans—dressed in wool, linen, and leather, as the cotton of India was a curiosity that only naturalists had heard of; silk, imported along the Silk Road from China, was an extravagant luxury.

England was the big wool player of the 1200s and guarded her wool empire furiously. In 1275 Edward I imposed an export tax on wool called the "Great Custom" and even dictated that wool was to be used in all burials. "Owling" (smuggling cloth out of England) was at one time punishable by the cutting off of a hand. To top it off, in 1699, the English crown forbade its American colonies to trade wool with anyone but England herself.

The biggest profit in wool was to be found in the dyeing and finishing of the woven product. Each producer created their own "cottage industry" in which they provided the raw material and a cash advance to the individual makers. Once the artisan had produced the cloth within the strict guides and timelines agreed, they were paid the remainder of their fee.

This cottage industry was swept away in the Industrial Revolution. With the introduction of mass production technology into wool and wool-cloth manufacturing, substantial mills (which were "dark" and "Satanic," if you're William Blake) were built—mostly in the north of England and in Wales. Villages and towns became prosperous—but only while the mills were open and busy. Of course, most of the English and Welsh mills closed as wool was replaced by man-made substitutes, and much of the wool production industry moved to other countries.

Today, of the one billion sheep in the world, only thirty million are to be found in Britain. The big sheep producers are Australia, New Zealand, and China, which hold seven hundred and seventy million sheep between them, with the remainder spread throughout Europe and the Americas.

Production

Sheep are usually shorn once a year in the spring or summer months, although in some places, such as South America, shearing may happen up to three times a year.

Wool is still put through the original cleaning and classification process to prepare it for weaving. Grease wool—wool straight off the sheep—contains lanolin, dirt, skin cells, and various other "interesting" particles. It is cleaned first by removing debris by hand and then washed in a soapy bath, with the lanolin extracted being passed on to the cosmetic industry. The clean wool is separated and the fluffy fleece set aside from the other, less valuable remnants.

The fleece is then sorted into varying qualities ready for different applications. The quality of wool is determined by the crimps, fiber diameter, color, and strength.

It's then processed in one of two ways:

Worsted—Uniform lengths of fine fibers are used. These are carded, combed, and formed into strands, then spun into smooth fabric. It's a superior cloth and used for fine clothing and interiors textiles.

Woolens—These are the short fibers, which are loosely spun, with a low to medium twist. They are softer and fuzzier than the fibers used for worsted wool. Woolens are generally bulkier and heavier than worsteds and are made into sturdier wools such as heavy tweeds, textured wools, and coatings.

Recycled wool is made by cutting or tearing apart existing wool fabric and then re-spinning it. This makes the wool fibers shorter and of lower quality than the original cloth. It is often mixed with raw wool or cotton to make an acceptable cloth.

Uses

In addition to clothing, wool has been used for blankets, horse rugs, saddle cloths, carpeting, felt, wool insulation, and upholstery. Its uses are myriad—wool felt covers piano hammers, and Roman legionnaires used breastplates made of wool felt.

It can be woven into a fine scarf or a firm tartan kilt, a chunky tweed suit, or a tightly upholstered wool felt sofa. Every country has specific uses, but it is safe to assume that wool can be used almost everywhere—from a knitted iPad cover to cashmere curtains.

Types of Wool Cloth

Not an exhaustive list—but a good start.

Angora—The downy coat produced by the Angora rabbit, it is known for its softness, thin fibers, and what knitters refer to as a halo (fluffiness). It is also known for its silky texture, with feels similar to fur. It is much warmer and lighter than wool due to the hollow core of the fibers. Angora is normally blended with wool to give the yarn elasticity.

Cashmere—Sourced specifically from the necks of goats. The word cashmere derives from an old spelling of Kashmir, a region in northern India/Pakistan. It's also known as *pashmina*, an Urdu word meaning wool. It is fine in texture—strong, light, and soft—and garments made from it provide excellent insulation. Cashmere is most recognizable in woolen shawls, but can be found in everything from knitwear to coats and curtains.

Felt—A nonwoven cloth that is produced by applying pressure or friction to hot, wet wool. While some types of felt are very soft, others are tough enough to form construction materials. Felt can be of any color, and made into any shape or size. Felt-making is still practiced by the Altaic people in Central and East Asia, who use it to make rugs, tents, clothing, and yurts. Closer to home, felt is often used for a creative expression in textile art and design.

Tweed—This is a rough, unfinished fabric with a soft, open, flexible texture. It is made in either plain or twill weave and may have a check or herringbone pattern. Harris Tweed is handwoven by the islanders on the Isles of Harris, Lewis, Uist, and Barra in the Outer Hebrides of Scotland, using their local wool. Like the Outer Hebrides, Donegal in Ireland has also been producing tweed from local materials for hundreds of years. Sheep thrive in the hills and bogs of Donegal, and indigenous plants such as blackberries, fuchsia, gorse (whins), and moss provide the dyes.

Tartan—This is made with alternating bands of colored (pre-dyed) wool threads woven as both warp and weft at right angles to each other. They form visible diagonal lines where the different colors cross, which give the appearance of new colors blended from the original ones. Until the middle of the 19th century, the Highland tartans were associated with either regions or districts, rather than any specific clan—even if movies tell us otherwise! Tartan designs were produced by local weavers for local tastes and would be colored using natural dyes available in that area.

Wool bouclé—Made famous by Coco Chanel, this is a loosely woven or knitted fabric that has small curls, which make the surface nubbly. It's a very "easy" fabric and was the conduit cloth for Chanel to create her simple unstructured designs, as clothing could be cut simply and without rigorous structure.

Wool flannel—A soft, woven fabric of varying fineness. It can be brushed to create extra softness or remain unbrushed. It has either a single- or double-sided nap. Flannel is commonly used to make tartan, bedding, and sleepwear. It has been made since the 17th century in Wales in various weights and forms since the 17th century, but is possibly most remembered as the cloth for the white trousers of early cricketers.

Dip-Dyed Wool Gauze Panel

Throughout *Cloth*, you'll notice that I like to dye fabric using natural dyes. For me this is about balancing heavily patterned cloth such as quilts, rugs, or embroidery with a far simpler handcrafted textile. It balances out rooms and also brings a lightness to the way we dress. We have access to so many handmade fabrics from around the world that it seems only right to present them in their simplest form and to celebrate them. They are often very humble fabrics used for linings or undergarments. Yet, if you use them generously and in the spirit in which they were created, they can be incredibly beautiful.

The fabric I have used for this project is an organic wool gauze, woven in India. It's handwoven, slightly flecked, and feels delightful. I used wool because I wanted something multifunctional—a curtain panel to provide privacy, yet let the light in; a lightweight blanket to wrap around you in bed, or a scarf when it's a little chilly outside.

Wool absorbs dye wonderfully and so with a combination of handmade cloth and Mother Nature's ingredients, I think you can make an item of real beauty.

Finished Size

Any size—but at least 80in. in length

Materials

- 87–118in. of handwoven wool gauze or lightweight wool—ivory or undyed in color. Wool gauze is usually 35–47in. in width.
- Natural dye in a color of your choice (see pages 15–17 for more information on natural dyeing)
- 100 percent cotton thread (optional)

Other Tools

- Iron and ironing board
- One or two plastic buckets or storage bins
- Metal-headed pins

Prepare

Prewash the wool on a cool wash to eliminate any shrinkage and remove any finishes that resist dye. Dry, then press with a warm iron. I didn't hem the panel as I liked the raw edges. You can hem if you would like, or run a line of stitching along each cut end to prevent excessive raveling. Use 100 percent cotton thread if you want to do this. When you are ready to dye, cold rinse the fabric again and wring out any excess moisture.

Dye

Now the fun bit! Go to pages 15–17 to read through the section on natural dyes. Choose a plant, tea, or powdered dye of your choice. Create your dye using the relevant fixatives. You can start with a small amount of dye and test the color with scraps of wool if you desire. If it's too dark, just add some more boiling water. If it's too light, just add more dye. This dip-dye method can be a little messy, so move out-of-doors if you can or to an area in which it is fine to make a mess.

Fill a bucket with the dye mix until the liquid is at least 8in. deep. Decide where you want the top of the dyed bands to be and use pins to mark this line on both ends of the cloth. Pin both ends together so that you can dye them at the same time. ▣ Hold your fabric as straight as possible and dip into the bucket to just below the pin line. Don't dip the pins as the fabric draws the color a little higher. ▣ Keep the fabric in the dye until it turns the color you want it to be—bear in mind that it will dry a little lighter. Rinse the fabric downward—in other words, away from the undyed section—in cold water to remove excess dye until the water runs clear. ▣ Either hang to dry outside or protect the floor inside with newspaper and hang to dry.

Design Thoughts

You can create a multitude of effects with these panels through your choice of fabric, dye color, and technique.

You can use wool, linen, cotton, or silk gauze/loose-weave cloth for these panels, depending on the look and feel that you want. Wool and silk will "take" the dye more readily as they are animal-based fibers, whereas linen and cotton plant-based fibers will give you a lighter color from the same dye concentration.

Each fabric will come as a different base color. They may have been bleached white or left in their natural creamy state. If you don't want the middle section to remain ivory/white, you can base dye the whole panel a light tea color (use the tea-staining method from the Tea-Stained Silk Drawstring Bags—see pages 114–117), or you could choose two or three contrasting shades for a more dramatic feel. Dye each color individually, letting the fabric dry before you move on to the next color.

If you want to dye each end a different color, you can do this at the same time with two separate buckets, or take it in stages—it depends on how good you are at multitasking!

You can add to this project by creating an ombré effect. Create several pin lines with rows of pins at least 4in. apart. Once you have dyed the first section, remove the first set of pins and add more boiling water to dilute the dye. Dip the wool again, to just below the second pin line. Wait and then remove these pins. Add a little more water and move up to just below the third pin line, and so on. This graduates the color from dark to light without sharp lines. This is always very beautiful.

This project can, of course, be adjusted to make curtains, blankets, or bed throws as well as scarves and wraps. You can mix in the shibori techniques shown with the Tie-Dye Shawl (see pages 106–109) and you can make this any color and size you like. Whatever you choose, it will be glorious.

Wool Pet Bed

Dog owners have lower blood pressure and suffer less anxiety than people of a similar age who don't have a dog. Strange fact—but true. The "accidents" and occasional displays of what we humans refer to as "naughtiness" are quickly forgotten when you watch them sleep, stroke them, or see them run and play. Pets love us unconditionally and give us a sense of contentment and utter joy. You may be a cat lover, a dog lover, or a hamster lover. It doesn't really matter—you know how they make you feel.

I have two dogs (and wish I had more) so I have hunted for beds that are both comfortable for them and aesthetically pleasing for me. In summer they often stretch out on a cool floor, but in winter they want comfort and warmth.

I've used vintage kilim rugs as rugs, of course, but also as pillows. They are wonderfully tactile and warm, and are usually woven in handsome color combinations. I thought the rugs would be perfect to turn into beds that would be both comfortable for our dogs and attractive for our home.

Finished Size

- Small   25½in. (terrier)
- Medium   35½in. (small spaniel)
- Large   45in. (labrador)
- Seam allowances are ⅜in. and are included in the cutting sizes.
- To work out the correct size bed for your pet, measure them from the nose to the base of the tail when they are lying down fully stretched, and choose the size up from that measurement. I've made the beds circular, as dogs and cats also like to sleep curled up and a circular bed seems to work better for this project.

Materials

- 1 whole or part of a vintage kilim rug—you can pick these up at fairs or online for a very reasonable price
- 16–24in. contrasting wool or cotton for the sides
- 28–47in. sturdy cotton or linen in a neutral to dark tone, for the bottom of the bed. Most cotton or linen will come in widths of 45–57in.
- 100 percent cotton thread in a neutral color to match the tone of the rug
- Your chosen filling—this can be polyester, old feather pillows, blankets, or beanbag filling. It's up to you and what your dog finds comfortable.
- 1 zipper—a minimum of 22in. long

Other Tools

- Iron and ironing board
- Long ruler—at least 24in. long
- Tailor's chalk or dressmaker's pencil
- Pins
- Fabric scissors
- Sewing machine with zipper foot

Prepare

Make sure that your kilim rug is clean—you can either hand wash it or have it dry-cleaned. ◻ Prewash the fabric for the sides and bottom of the bed on a warm wash to eliminate any shrinkage. Dry, then press with a hot iron. ◻ You need to make a simple pattern using newspaper or cardboard. Draw a circle 26in., 36in., or 45in. in diameter on the paper or cardboard. If your pet is larger or smaller than the suggested sizes, then create a circle to fit. Fold the circle in half and trace the half on a separate piece of paper. Add ⅜in. along the straight edge—this will be the seam allowance for the zipper. Measure the circumference of the circle, add 1½in. to this measurement, then halve it. This will give you the required length of the side panel. Create a pattern 5½in. in height by the final length measurement. You will have three pattern pieces—top (circle), bottom (half-circle), and side (rectangle).

Cut

Using weights or pins, secure the top pattern piece to the kilim rug. Make sure that you are happy with the position as the rug will probably have different stripes or markings. Cut one piece using very sharp fabric scissors. ◻ Then, using the bottom pattern piece, cut two from the cotton or linen. Using the side pattern piece, cut two from the wool or cotton.

Sew

Start with your bottom pieces. Fold and press a ⅜in. seam allowance on the two straight edges. ◻ Turn the two strips of the fabric right side up and pin the folded edges to each side of the zipper, centering it in the middle of the fabric. Use the zipper foot on your sewing machine and sew all the way along both sides to secure the zipper. ◻ Change back to the standard sewing foot on your machine. Unzip the zipper halfway. Pin the remaining fabric together and sew a ⅜in. seam at both ends. Press the seams. ◻ Sew the two side pieces together at both short edges so that you have created a circle. Press the seams open. ◻ Pin the side to the bottom, right sides facing. Make sure you align the side seams with the center seam of the bottom. Sew together and press the seams open. ◻ Repeat this with the top kilim panel. Steam press the seams open and turn right side out. ◻ Topstitch along the top and bottom edges of the side panel for a sharper finish. Press along the seams one last time.

Fill the bed with your stuffing of choice, and your pet's bed is complete.

Design Thoughts

Many pet beds are made of cotton and polyester so that they can be thrown in the washing machine which is incredibly practical. Kilim are better hand washed or dry-cleaned (or even beaten like a rug), so if this seems too much, you can change the top to wool that has been prewashed to avoid shrinkage or a sturdy warm cotton such as denim or upholstery-weight linen. Whatever fabric you choose, it does need to be robust as cats like to scratch and dogs like to "dig" their beds.

You can use all one fabric or three, although two pieces of kilim will be too thick to sew together using a home sewing machine. Use a contrast thread on your topstitching to pick out a particular color in the kilim or something in the room where your pet sleeps.

Wool Felt Oven Gloves

Wool felt is a wonderful textile. It was probably the first cloth created by man and yet, until recently, it seems to have been relegated to children's crafting projects. Thankfully, we are now seeing the rise of a more artisanal cloth that is both visually and physically inspiring. It's now also being used in many different ways—from gorgeous toys to smart homewares and furniture—even in insightful industrial applications.

You can buy felted wool in soft natural colors as well as the bright primary palette we all know. Some felt is a by-product of industrial goods. Other products are hand-felted by an artisan. Or you can use felt you have recycled from woolen garments. As a cloth it's a great protector, is heat- and moisture-resistant, and, most importantly, it's now really rather attractive.

Finished Size

- 13¾in. × 8¼in.
- Seam allowances are ⅜in. and are included in the pattern pieces.

Materials

- You will need a piece of wool felt approx. 20in. × 16in. per glove. Make sure the felt is at least ⅛in. thick—the thicker the cloth, the more heat resistant it is.
- 100 percent cotton thread in a matching color

Other Tools

- Fabric scissors
- Tailor's chalk or dressmaker's pencil
- Pins
- Sewing machine
- Ruler

Prepare

Cut out or trace the oven glove pattern piece provided in the back of the book.

Cut

Using weights or pins, secure the pattern piece to the felt. Trace around it and cut. Cut two pieces (a front and a back) per glove. Wool felt has no right or wrong side.

Sew

Pin the glove together and sew around it, leaving the bottom open. Trim around the seams to ¼in. and trim any excess thread. That's it, your oven glove is complete.

Design Thoughts

Wool felt is a great cloth to use when you need protection from heat, knocks, or scratches. It's perfect for an iPad or phone cover and could also be used for many items in the kitchen to absorb heat and water. It works well for everything from pot trivets to placemats and coasters. The list is almost endless. You can create your own felt from purposely shrinking your old sweaters or cardigans in a hot washing machine and tumble drier. You've probably done it accidentally—I think it might be quite satisfying to do it on purpose!

Wool Overnight Bag

Going on a trip, a quick getaway, or a last-minute booking by the sea? Traveling is often at the heart of our storytelling. "Do you remember that market/restaurant/mountain/beach?" I have an ivory leather overnight bag that has been with me on many travels. I had it made years ago as I wanted something unique—something that would look different from everything else tumbling around the baggage carousel. Something that said "This is me and my travels." Once that bag arrives, you can relax (because those minutes waiting at the carousel are fairly torturous) and get on with the business of travel and adventure.

Finished Size

- 17in. × 13in. × 51in.
- Seam allowances are ⅜in. and are included in the cutting sizes and pattern pieces.

Materials

- 1yd sturdy wool fabric—wool is usually 51–57in. in width
- 1yd lining fabric
- 1yd firm fusible interfacing
- 1 pair of leather handles with fittings
- 24in. zipper with metal teeth
- 100 percent cotton thread in a matching tone to the wool
- 2 x strips (⅛in. x 10in) leather, wool or lining scraps

Other tools

- Pins
- Tailor's chalk or dressmaker's pencil
- Fabric scissors
- Iron and ironing board
- Sewing machine with zipper foot

Prepare

Trace or cut out the pattern pieces from the back of the book. You will cut the main body, top panel, and center panel.

Cut

Pin or weight the pattern pieces to the fabric and cut out the fabric as per the instructions on the pattern pieces. Transfer all markings. Cut out the interfacing panels.
- Iron the wool panels to the interfacing—making sure the fabric's wrong side is facing the interfacing.

Sew the Bag Outer

To insert the zipper, place it face down on the right side of one of the top panels and pin it in place. ⊡ Put the zipper foot on your sewing machine and stitch the zipper to the fabric. Repeat for the second top panel. Press the seam and clip any loose threads. ⊡ Change back to a normal foot. Topstitch down each side of the zipper on the right side of the fabric. ⊡ Pin and sew the two center panels together at one end, right sides facing. Press the seams open and topstitch down each side of the seam. ⊡ Pin and sew the two ends of the center panel to the ends of the top panel. You will be forming a loop. Press the seams open and topstitch along the center panel side of the seam. ⊡ Transfer the handle positions from the pattern pieces to the main panel with pins or chalk. Attach the bag handles according to the supplier's instructions. ⊡ Pin one main panel to the center/top loop, right sides facing. Make sure you line up the markings. Sew together. Open the zipper halfway and repeat with the second main panel. Press the seams and clip the corners. Turn right side out through the open zipper and press the seams again.

Sew the Bag Lining

To make the pocket, turn over ³⁄₈in. to the wrong side of the fabric and press. Turn over another ³⁄₄in. and press. Topstitch this seam closed. ☐ Pin the pocket to one of the main panels, with the wrong side of the pocket facing the right side of the panel. Stitch down the center of the pocket so that you have made two channels. ☐ On each of the top panels, fold over ³⁄₈in. to the wrong side of the fabric and press. ☐ You now need to make the lining in the same way as the outer, without the zipper. Make sure you capture the pocket pieces when pinning and sewing the main panels to the center panels. ☐ When you have completed the lining, leave the lining bag wrong side out. ☐ To finish the bag, slip the lining inside the outer and pin together at the zipper. Slip stitch the lining to the outer on the outside of the zipper.

Create the zip pull

Gather strips of leather, or use scraps from your wool or your lining fabric. Although there are no set measurements, I cut two strips ¹⁄₈in. x 10in., using leftover leather from one of the hide projects. ☐ Use a rotary cutter and mat if you have one, or mark the measurements in pencil and then cut with sharp scissors. ☐ Thread both strips through the hole in the zip pull and tie into a knot.

Let the traveling commence.

Design Thoughts

There is an almost never-ending number of ways to personalize this design. Obviously, you can use any sturdy fabric. Add another pocket if needed. This bag would be great in waxed cotton—more utilitarian but very stylish. I have suggested leather handles, as I think these will wear better, but you could make fabric handles or use very firm webbing instead. Suppliers listed in the Resources section on page 185 provide all sorts of zippers, clips, studs, and handles for bag-making, which means that you can create a completely unique bag—which I believe is the whole point of this project anyway.

Vintage Wool Blanket Pillows

There is a comforting sturdiness to vintage blankets. It's a given that they have been made well, as was the one used to make the pillows shown here, so they are still thick, warm, and softened from decades of use. From picnics, to camping, to whiling away an afternoon at the beach, blankets have always been used to keep us dry, warm, and comfortable. They are more robust than a quilt and carry an ample whiff of adventure about them. You can pick them up fairly cheaply from all types of sellers. Old military blankets come in great greige palettes or you could look for Welsh plaid or woven blankets. These pillows make a great "second" pillow on your bed or are a good alternative shape for a sofa pillow.

Finished Size

- 20in. × 30in.
- Seam allowances are ³⁄₈in. and are included in the cutting sizes.

Materials

- 1 vintage wool blanket
- Cotton fabric—to make two pillows you will need 43in. cotton fabric that is approx. 42¹⁄₂–45in. wide.
- 100 percent cotton thread in a color to match the blanket

Other Tools

- 20in. × 29¹⁄₂in. feather and down pillow forms
- Long ruler—at least 24in. long
- Tailor's chalk or dressmaker's pencil
- Fabric scissors
- Pins
- Sewing machine

Prepare

Make sure that the blanket is clean—dry clean or hand wash if needed.

Cut

Backing Cut the cotton fabric into two 20¹⁄₂in. strips. Fold each strip in half widthwise and cut in two. You should have four pieces of fabric 20¹⁄₂in. × approx. 21–22¹⁄₂in.

Front Look at the fabric and decide if there are any patterns or motifs you would like centered or positioned on a certain part of the pillow. My blanket had a double white strip woven down the center. I wanted this to be in the middle of each of my pillows, so I based my marking points from this. Measure and mark two rectangles 20¹⁄₂in. × 28¹⁄₄in. Cut out using sharp scissors.

Sew the Pillow Backs

On the short edge of one back piece, turn over ³⁄₈in. to the wrong side and press. Turn over again ³⁄₄in., press, and pin in place. Topstitch this in either one or two rows, depending on the look you like. Repeat this for all pillow backs.

Sew the Pillow

Place a pillow front right side up. Take one pillow back and place it right side down, on top of the pillow front, with the raw edges matching. The topstitched edge should be toward the center. ▢ Place a second pillow back right side down, with the raw edges matching. ▢ You should have an overlap of the two topstitched edges. This is called an envelope closure. ▢ Pin the top and two backs together, making sure you pin through all three layers when necessary. ▢ Sew around all four edges using a $^3/_8$in. seam allowance. ▢ Press the seams open and trim the corners. ▢ Turn the pillow right side out and gently push out the corners to make them sharp. Press again.

Insert a pillow form, and you're done.

Design Thoughts

Woolen blankets come in every color and weave. They also tell stories. You can find military blankets from almost every country online—some are new, many others have history. Vintage Welsh woolen blankets are increasingly sought after as they show such wonderful technical skill. As many of the mills are now closed, they become increasingly valuable in every sense. If you can find an old damaged Welsh blanket, then this is a great way to preserve a bit of textile history. These blankets and the fabric are still being woven today, so you can often pick up the wool as yardage rather than a finished blanket (thereby avoiding cutting up a finished blanket if that bothers you).

A pair of pillows made out of Scottish plaid blankets would be a grand statement. You could contrast it with the linen used for the Linen Comforter Cover and Pillowcases (see pages 172–175) to create a really tactile bedroom. There are blankets currently being produced from recycled wool remnants. These come in a huge array of colors, are really well priced, and would be most cheery.

You can use any wool fabric for the pillows if you don't want to cut up a blanket—it's just about having a different texture and warmth in the mix of your home. Plain cashmere or a soft bouclé would feel luxurious, whereas wool suiting fabric would be smooth and minimalist.

You can, of course, change the size of the pillow or construct it in the same way as the Linen Pillowcases (see pages 172–175) so that it is more of a pillowcase.

Finally, you could add extra embellishment through embroidery or creative stitching to contrast the masculine feel of the blanket and choose either subtle or contrasting fabrics for the back as a last decorative flourish.

Wool Ottoman

Not a pillow, not a chair, but a very handy resting place for feet, small children, pets, or a lovely tray of coffee and cookies. An ottoman is that incredibly useful piece of furniture that fills the void between sofa and floor. They can be stored under coffee tables to be pulled out at a moment's notice for extra guests or as a place to rest your half-read novels. Put them in your children's rooms for them to roll about and daydream on, or give them to someone who is just starting on their own story of home. They are a win-win piece of furniture and yet simple to create. Although they can be made out of any upholstery-weight fabric, wool makes them soft and comforting, as well as very durable.

Finished Size

- 12in. (h) × 26in. (w)
- The seam allowances are ³⁄₈in. and are included in the pattern pieces.

Materials

- You will need approx. 2yds upholstery-weight fabric, dependent on its width
- Stuffing—you have several options: leftover fabric scraps, polyester stuffing, or beanbag filling. Fabric will make the ottoman heavy to move, but it will be firm. Polyester stuffing and beanbag filling are easy to source and light to use, but will need constant topping up. Alternatively, you can always use old feather pillow forms or comforters that are past their best for sleeping on. Leave them in their outers rather than cutting them open, as the feathers will go everywhere.
- Sewing thread—100 percent cotton all-purpose thread is best—in a color to match the fabric
- Embroidery silk thread in a color of your choice

Other Tools

- Tailor's chalk or dressmaker's pencil
- Fabric scissors
- Pins
- Sewing machine
- Iron and ironing board
- Long ruler—at least 24in. long

Prepare

Cut out or trace the ottoman pattern provided in the back of the book.

Cut

Cut eight long panels and two central panels, making sure you transfer the dots and crosses on the pattern pieces to your fabric, too.

Sew

Pin and sew together two of the long panels at side B, right sides together. Repeat this until you have joined four pieces. Press the seams open with a warm iron.
- Take two of the four panels and pin together along sides C and D. Sew together, making sure you pivot at each dot. Press the seams open, making sure that you really get into the corners. Clip around the seams if this makes it easier. ▫ Repeat this with another two panels and then join these two sections together. You have now made half of the ottoman.

▫ Repeat this process with the other four panels. Now you have two halves. ▫ Pin two sides of each half together, with the right sides together, but leave a gap of approx. 16in. in length on one of the edges. This is so you can stuff the ottoman. Sew together, making sure you pivot at the dots. Press your last seams. ▫ Turn right side out and stuff with your chosen filling until it is as firm as you want. Pin the opening together and slip-stitch closed. ▫ Fold over ⅜in. of your top panels to the wrong side. Press these down, so that you have a smaller hexagonal top with no raw edges showing. Take one top and pin it to the center of the ottoman (where all the seams have joined) wrong side down. Take care and line up the edges to the lines of each section. Sew your top panel to your ottoman using the embroidery silk thread. I used a simple slip-stitch but you could use a blanket or any other decorative stitch. Repeat this for the bottom of the ottoman.

You're done—put your feet up.

Design Thoughts

Ottomans are a great project to use vintage blankets on, or offcuts of hard-wearing Harris tweed. You can also use any upholstery-weight cloth, so if floral linen is more your thing, then this project would be a great piece to use it for. Go for variety in your children's rooms by using old Indian kantha quilts—you can often pick these up quite cheaply and cut around any damaged sections. You could also make these out of soft lambskin or any leather that you can sew on your machine—a little like a Moroccan ottoman. If you do use leather, don't fold over the raw edges of the top sections, and use an awl to create holes to stitch through.

The Organic Movement

We all love our vintage and antique fabrics. Finding and buying them is always interesting and we generally know the provenance of them. However, when we buy new clothes or textiles for our homes, we don't often think about how the raw materials are grown or where they have come from. Regrettably, it isn't always good, so here are a few facts and figures that may be useful.

Approximately 25 percent of the world's insecticides and 10 percent of the world's pesticides are used on conventionally grown cotton and it is estimated that 50 percent of all the insecticide used in India is sprayed on cotton. This causes monumental damage to the environment and to the health of farm laborers who are exposed to the chemicals. Nonorganic fabric can also use genetically modified seeds—that's right—genetically modified seeds. . .

Unfortunately it gets worse: As the pests develop resistance to these chemicals and the soil loses its fertility, the farmers find themselves trapped in a never-ending spiral of debt. Farmers who farm nonorganic cotton may have to borrow from local moneylenders to buy the chemicals they need to grow their cotton. As the crops continue to dwindle, the debt continues to grow. Extensive illness, depression, and a significant number of suicides among cotton farmers can be the very sad consequence.

These are perhaps not the facts and figures one wants to read in a book on beautiful cloth. But knowledge is power and you can make better choices where possible.

So, on to the good stuff. Organic cotton farming offers an environmentally and economically sustainable option. It uses natural fertilizers and pheromone traps instead of the unpleasant pesticides—crops are rotated and bugs are hand-picked. Weeding is also done by hand and pests are controlled using biological and natural methods, such as other insects that are their natural enemies. This allows farmers to grow their own food safely and keep animals as well as grow healthy crops. They receive more for their crop, their crops are more consistent, and the input costs are lower.

Many African farmers control 4 to 5 acres, which although is not as large as the farms in developed countries, it is enough to farm organically, allowing them and their families to live a more prosperous, resilient, and healthy life. There are increased opportunities for women working within the organic system, who are often not permitted to own land and grow conventional cotton. Also there is an international support structure that ensures the health and well-being of all farmers irrelevant of sex. The farmers involved also gain skills and training because the organic system is so tightly controlled and education-focused. And lastly, because of these tight controls, the farmers are generally paid faster than those in the traditional industry, so that the cycle can continue at a profitable and healthy pace for all.

Apart from all of the these facts and figures (and I know it is a bit serious), I've always found that organic cotton just looks and feels better. It's good in spirit as well as construction and, as a raw material (fabric), it is often the same or of a similar price to traditional cotton—a win-win situation in all ways.

Although still only a small percentage of all cotton farming, organic production is growing, with China, the United States, India, Pakistan, Brazil, Turkey, Greece, Australia, Syria, Mali, and Egypt all producing organic cotton. It's continuing to grow and I'm sure it won't be long before organic is truly the mainstay.

The deity

The deity of the fabric world must surely be silk. It is both beautiful and luxurious, but also created without the intervention of man—divine indeed. No other cloth seems to garner the same emotive reaction as silk. It is haute couture for some and a pocket square for others. It connotes weddings, births, and all special occasions. It is beauty, history, and modernity, and in the cloth world we seem to covet nothing more than silk. It is fluid and delicate like no other and holds color so that it looks almost luminous. It has clothed royalty since 27 BC and its secrets were revealed on the Silk Road. It has been everything, from currency and curtains, to tapestries and ties, to parachutes and pantyhose.

Silk is a unique cloth as it is spun into existence by the silkworm, ready-made and in one length, so delicate that it needs to be twisted into stranded lengths to make it strong enough to weave. Yet it is the strongest natural fiber—a steel filament of the same diameter will break before silk does. But it is also temperamental under sunlight and doesn't respond positively to mankind's perspiration.

Silk is now made wherever silkworms flourish—they like temperate climates in which white-berried mulberry trees grow. China, India, eastern Italy, and southern France have all had a long association with silk. Other countries such as England and the United States have tried, but with limited success or, perhaps, desire, as they were so busy and successful with cotton.

Silk was discovered in China and was a closely guarded secret for centuries. Folklore says that silk finally left China in the hair of a princess promised to a prince of Khotan. She refused to go without the fabric she loved, thereby delivering silk and its secrets to the world.

Silk is a natural protein fiber, very similar to human hair. It starts life as a liquid, which then hardens on contact with air. It mostly comes from the cocoons of the mulberry silkworm, which are now reared in captivity—a process called sericulture. Silk fabric shimmers because of the fiber's prismlike structure. This means the fabric can refract light, which is why the finished cloth often looks like it is made of many colors—miraculous.

The worm creates a cocoon in which it pupates and covers itself in silk thread. Regrettably, as with all natural fibers, there is a cost. In order to use the silk in its strongest and most luxuriant form, the pupae have to be killed while inside the cocoon. This is done by either dipping them into boiling water, or by piercing them with a needle. Unlike with other natural fibers, there is no need for chemicals, or a huge strain on natural resources with silk production. If you don't want to buy silk that has been created through sericulture, there is wild silk—or Tussah silk. To create this cloth, silk cocoons are gathered in the wild rather than through concentrated farming. The pupae have usually left the cocoon, thereby tearing the thread into shorter lengths. As a cloth it has a slubby feel, and is usually left in its natural color as it doesn't take dye well—it's still very beautiful though.

Although silk is one of the strongest natural fibers, it loses up to 20 percent of its strength when wet. It doesn't have great elasticity, which is why it is often cut on the bias. It is weakened and can rot if exposed to too much sunlight. If you let it get dirty, insects like to make a meal of it and, as mentioned above, it doesn't like sweat. It is very partial to static cling and can shrink substantially dependent on the weave. There are good reasons why we use silk as a luxury good rather than an everyday fabric.

History

According to Chinese tradition, sericulture began in 27 BC. China perfected the art of breeding silkworms to get the maximum production of thread from each cocoon. Only women were allowed to breed the worms, and most workers in all stages of the process were female. The right to wear silk was reserved for the Emperor and the highest echelon. As silk became more and more valuable it was used as currency and as a reward, rather than just clothing.

The earliest evidence of silk dates back to between 3,000 BC and 4,000 BC, with other fragments being recovered from royal tombs from around the time of the Shang Dynasty.

Silk cloth stayed a Chinese secret until the Silk Road opened during the latter half of the first millennium BC. The Chinese used the route as a means to export cloth only—the wondrous worms were still hidden away.

Eventually, Korea, Japan, and India discovered how to harness the wonders of the silkworm. Then the Byzantines managed to obtain a few eggs, closely followed by Arab countries. In Islamic teachings, Muslim men are forbidden to wear silk, as it is believed that men should avoid clothing that could be considered feminine or extravagant.

Finally, the Crusades brought silk to Italy and key silk producers were created. Italy imported so much of the cloth from China that the enormous volume of gold leaving Rome resulted in silk clothing being regarded as decadent and debauched. To this day it has a sensuous and indulgent quality like no other fabric.

France joined Italy in production, though most other Western countries failed to develop a successful silk industry of their own. Huguenot exiles arrived in London's Spitalfields, where they made beautiful silk. But the damp and cool British climate prevented silk production from being anything but a purely domestic trade.

James I tried to establish silk production in England in the early 17th century by planting 100,000 mulberry trees near Hampton Court Palace. Unfortunately he purchased the wrong kind of tree and both the worms and the idea died.

With the arrival of the Industrial Revolution everything changed again. Cotton became the prevalent cloth, and silk became even more of a luxury product. The mechanical developments of industrialization did very little for silk, as it was already a spun fiber. Weaving was still an incredibly skilled process and could not be sped up by machines.

An epidemic of silkworm diseases followed and production continued to fall, with France being a major casualty.

World War II interrupted the silk trade from Japan, so as silk prices increased, man-made fibers were introduced to take their place.

Silk is still produced in Thailand, Vietnam, and India, but China is now once again the world's largest producer of silk. It is of course still a luxury product, and I imagine it will remain so for a very long time.

Production

Sericulture, or farmed silk, is a different process from wild silk, as man controls every step. As the vast majority of silk comes from sericulture, it's probably best to understand this process. But you might prefer to skip this section if you don't want to know about it.

Silk moths lay their eggs on a special type of paper. Once the silk-worms hatch, they are fed fresh mulberry leaves—an enormous amount of mulberry leaves, as 3,000 silkworms need to eat 100lb of leaves to make 1lb of silk fiber. . .

After about 35 days the silkworms are around 10,000 times heavier than when they were hatched and are ready to begin spinning. Within a few days they have spun approximately 1 mile of silk and are completely encased. The silkworms are killed and the cocoons are soaked in boiling water to soften them. The fiber is unwound to produce one long continuous thread. As silk fiber is so fine, three to ten strands are spun together to form a single useful thread.

Sericulture has obviously drawn criticism from animal rights groups. Gandhi was opposed to it on the basis of the Ahimsa philosophy (not to hurt any living thing). Wild silk is an alternative, or using vintage or antique silk may be a more acceptable way for you to incorporate the cloth into your home if sericulture doesn't feel right.

Uses

Silk is best known as clothing for very special days or—in history—very important people. However, it has also been used for much humbler applications. Parachute silk was made from actual silk at one time, and silk has been used in gunpowder bags, medical thread, bicycle tires, and comforter fillers, among many other practical uses.

Like all natural fibers, its absorbency keeps you cool in hot weather and its low conductivity keeps warm air close to the skin during cold weather, so is perfect to wear all year round. As well as the all-important wedding dress and the couture ensembles of our forefathers, silk can be used for most clothing, lingerie, and gentlemen's neckties. Silk's luster and drape also make it perfect (but expensive) for curtains, rugs, bedding, and tapestries.

New developments in silk production have led to specialist silk underwear for those suffering with eczema, as well as for making everything from disposable cups to drug delivery systems to holograms.

Types of Silk

This list reads like an Edwardian haute couture order book (or TV period drama). Every weight, texture, or sheerness you can imagine:

Brocade—Brocade is a jacquard weave with an embossed effect and contrasting surfaces.

Charmeuse—The back of the fabric is a flattened crêpe while the front is a shimmery satin weave. It also has great drape.

Chiffon—The lightest and most diaphanous of the silks, it is also see-through.

Crêpe de Chine—A lightweight fabric made by twisting fibers clockwise and counterclockwise. These are then woven in a plain-weave fabric, in which the twisted fibers give crêpe its "pebbly" look and feel.

Dupioni—Dupioni is reeled from double cocoons nested together. The threads are uneven and irregular. Often seen in Mother-of-the-Bride ensembles.

Faille—A soft, ribbed silk with wider ribs than seen in grosgrain ribbon, faille is slightly glossy.

Georgette—A sheer crêpe silk, heavier than chiffon and with a crinkled surface.

Habotai—A plain-weave silk available in different weights. This fabric has the feel that most people identify as silk. There are various weights from light, used for linings, to heavy, used for shirts and dresses. It's sometimes called pongee or China silk.

Jacquard—Jacquard silks offer various woven patterns, using matte and reflective threads to create a light-and-dark effect in the fabric. Usually used for curtains or upholstery and often seen in grand historic homes.

Matelasse—Matelasse has raised woven designs, usually jacquard, with the appearance of being puckered or quilted.

Noil—Noil is made from the short fibers left after spinning, so it doesn't shine like many other silk fabrics. Noil looks similar to cotton and resists wrinkling.

Organza—Similar to cotton organdie, but see-through.

Peau de soie—A stout, soft silk with fine cross ribs that looks slightly corded. It is sometimes called paduasoy.

Poult de soie—Poult de soie has heavy cross ribs and is sometimes called faille taffeta.

Raw silk—Raw silk is any silk yarn or fabric that hasn't had the natural "gum" washed away. The fabric is stiff and dull and tends to attract dirt and odours.

Shantung—Shantung is usually made with cultivated silk warp yarns and heavier dupioni filling yarns. Depending on the filling yarn, shantung may be lustrous or dull. It has a firm, semicrisp handle.

Silk broadcloth—A plain-weave silk fabric in various weights; crisper than China silk and often used for shirting.

Silk satin—A satin weave with a plain back.

Silk velvet—A type of woven tufted fabric in which the cut threads are evenly distributed, with a short dense pile, giving it a distinctive feel. It can be 100 percent silk, or a mixture of silk and viscose.

Tussah—Tussah is made from the cocoons of wild silkworms. It has irregular thick and thin yarns, creating uneven surface and color.

Kimono Silk Quilt

Japanese silk is probably my greatest fabric love. The actual cloth is beautifully made and the colors, patterns, and designs can be stunning. They are often painted and embroidered as well as printed—this attention to detail and fineness is what I love about it.

I made my first ever quilts from vintage kimono silk and they are as beautiful today as when I first made them. Silk does fade and is a little more fragile than cotton, but I think the end result is worth it.

As well as the heavily patterned silk of more decorative kimonos, I also love the simpler haoris. These were originally designed to be worn over the kimono and can be found online or in markets very easily. I've chosen three plain haori for this quilt—the pieces are relatively small, so the pattern comes from the change in color.

Quilts do take time and patience. You can break this project down in stages and just do it bit by bit, as it is an easy design to come back to. Don't be overwhelmed—just enjoy the process.

Finished Size

- 83in. × 83in.
- Seam allowances are ³⁄₈in. and are included in the cutting sizes.

Materials

For the Quilt Top You will need three haori kimonos with their linings if possible, and a few extra silk scraps (approx. 6½ yards fabric).

For the Quilt Backing Approx. 5½yds fabric. The finished size should be 83 in. × 83in., so you can also use fabric leftovers to make the backing, or a sheet, or any other robust cotton.

For the Binding Approx. 20in. fabric. You can use fabric scraps from the quilt top if you have excess left over, or use this as an opportunity to introduce a new fabric.

Other Materials

- Batting of your choice, 83in. × 83in.
- Sewing thread—100 percent cotton all-purpose thread is best, in a neutral color
- Quilting thread—100 percent cotton quilting thread in a color to match or contrast the fabric of the quilt top

Other Tools

- Iron and ironing board
- Rotary cutter and cutting mat
- Fabric scissors
- Long, fine pins
- Sewing machine
- Masking tape
- Quilting needle

Prepare

This quilt is created with three different-sized strips. These are then pieced into six different-sized blocks. It is an incredibly simple quilt to make, especially if you break it down into stages. Use the illustration on page 105 to guide you through the process. ⊡ If you are using haoris or kimonos, unpick the seams, remove all loose threads, and press with a cool iron. You may need to give the fabric a gentle hand wash first to remove dust or age spots. Check the linings to see if they are robust enough to use, as some will be too thin.

Cut

Divide your pile of fabric roughly into two-thirds/one-third, making sure that you spread the different colors and patterns evenly. ⊡ From the larger pile, you will cut all your $16\frac{1}{2}$in. strips. From the smaller pile you will cut your $12\frac{1}{2}$in. and $8\frac{1}{2}$in. strips. If you find you have cut too many $16\frac{1}{2}$in. strips once you've sewn your blocks, you can always cut them down for the remaining smaller blocks.

⊡ Using your rotary cutter and cutting mat, cut your fabric into $16\frac{1}{2}$in.-long pieces. Then cut strips at random widths—fat, medium, and skinny. The exact width of each isn't important. You'll find a rhythm as you go. ⊡ Put these aside and then divide the remaining pile into two. Cut the first pile into $12\frac{1}{2}$in. strips and the second into $8\frac{1}{2}$in. strips using the same method. ⊡ If you prefer, you can cut and sew the $16\frac{1}{2}$in.-square blocks first, then move on to the $12\frac{1}{2}$in.-square blocks and finally the $8\frac{1}{2}$in.-square blocks. If you are limited on fabric, or a little unsure of how much to cut, this may work better for you.

Sew

There are six different block sizes to sew—refer to the illustration for the size and quantity you need of each. ⊡ Starting with block A, choose two $16\frac{1}{2}$in. strips from the pile of cut fabric. Pin and sew along one long edge with right sides together. Continue adding strips until the block is slightly wider than the required $16\frac{1}{2}$in. Press the seams open and trim all excess threads. Measure the pressed block and trim off any excess fabric. Use this excess to start your next block. ⊡ Work your way through your fabric, making the required number of blocks for each size—and remember to spread the colors and patterns evenly throughout. ⊡ When you have made all 39 blocks, you just need to piece together the rows to make up the finished quilt top.

Using the illustration as your guide, lay out the blocks to form the quilt design. You can use a bed or a floor, or even pin them to a wall if you have space. Take your time to get a composition you like—you can take pictures with your phone or camera as a reference. ⊡ Start with row 1 and piece together the seven blocks in the order they are shown on page 105. Make sure you sew with the right sides of the fabric together. Press the seams open and trim any excess thread. Work your way through each of the rows until you have pieced all six rows. Then pin and sew each of the rows together. Trim the threads and press—your quilt top is complete. ⊡ Now make your quilt backing. Sew your backing fabric together until you have a square at least 90in. × 90in., or 4in. larger than your quilt top, if you have adjusted the size.

Build the Quilt

Press your backing and lay it right side down on a hard and clean surface, such as a clean floor. Smooth out the backing carefully so that there are no creases and then, using long pieces of masking tape, tape the fabric down at points all the way around the sides (but not the corners, as this stretches the quilt), smoothing as you go. This holds the backing flat, taut, and square. ▣ Lay your batting on top, smoothing it out, matching it to the backing. If your batting is bigger than your backing, trim it down to match. ▣ Press your quilt top until it's perfect, doing a final check for any loose threads as you go. ▣ Lay the quilt top on the batting with the right side up, making sure it is square with the backing. ▣ You now need to hold the three layers together so that you can quilt. Use long, fine pins and starting from either the center or one side of the quilt, pin the quilt all over every 4–6in., smoothing as you go. Alternatively, you can run long basting stitches across the whole quilt—again in 4–6in. rows.

Finishing Your Quilt

Using your masking tape, lay lines across the quilt top in a pattern that you like. This can be diagonals, squares, or just straight lines. I created diagonal lines 6in. apart. This will be your stitching line. Using your quilting thread and quilting needle, simply hand stitch a running stitch through all three layers, along the edge of the masking tape. Once you have completed a line you can remove that piece of masking tape and any pins in that area. I usually start from one side and work into the center, and then start on the other side and work into the center.

Binding Your Quilt

Measure all four sides of your quilt and add another 6–8in. to get the length of binding required. ▣ Join all the strips together into a continuous length. Press the joined strip in half along its length, with wrong sides together. ▣ Leave about 4in. of the binding strip free. Then pin one raw edge of the binding to the edge of the quilt top, through all layers. Pin all the way around the quilt until you come back to the start. ▣ Machine stitch around the quilt. When you get to a corner, stop about $\frac{1}{4}$in. from the edge of the corner, backstitch, and then fold the binding around the corner. Then continue sewing. ▣ When you get near the beginning, backstitch and remove the quilt from the sewing machine. ▣ Trim off the excess binding, fold the remaining binding over to the back of the quilt, and pin. Then hand-stitch the binding to the back of the quilt using a slip-stitch so that it is invisible.

Phew! It's done.

Design Thoughts

Silk is a very luxurious fabric to use for a quilt, which I love. However, if you want to make the quilt a little more robust, you can use cotton, or mix the two fabrics together, as I do in most of my quilts. Here I have used three tonal fabrics with a few scraps in much sharper shades, but you can use any palette you want. The quilt would be stunning in neutral shades or really fun in a vibrant clash of colors—it's up to you.

This is a great design for using up scraps, as you only have to have pieces a maximum of $16\frac{1}{2}$in. long and of any width.

On the back you can use cotton or linen. I used a vintage floral sheet, but you could use anything from antique linen to African wax cloth.

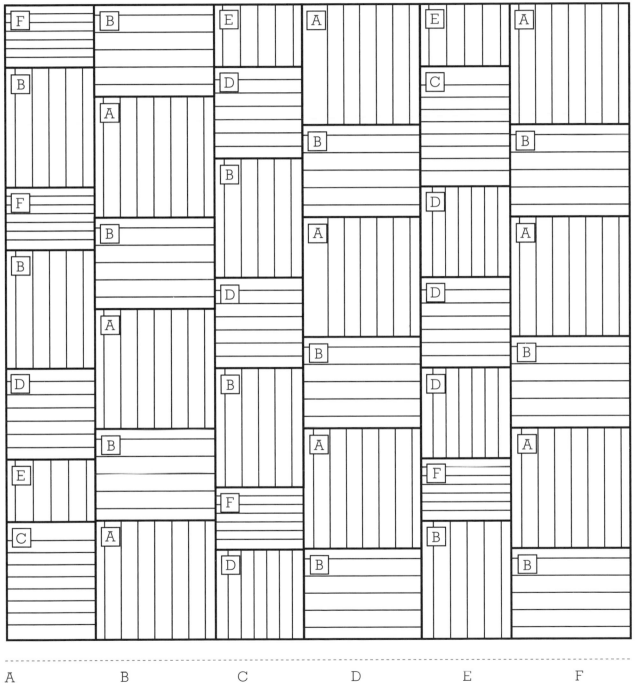

A
16½ × 16½in.
Panels × 9

B
16½ × 12½in.
Panels × 4

C
12½ × 16½in.
Panels × 2

D
12½ × 12½in.
Panels × 7

E
8½ × 12½in.
Panels × 3

F
12½ × 8½in.
Panels × 4

Tie-Dye Shawl

Tie-dyeing is a resist technique. Fabric is cinched and wrapped so that, when it's immersed in dye, certain areas resist the dye. The undyed areas form decorative patterns against the dyed ones.

Until recently, tie-dye probably didn't conjure the most stylish of images. But by using a more neutral color palette and a streamlined technique, you can create very beautiful tie-dyed garments or homewares. It's very simple to do and possibly a touch addictive once you've started.

Finished Size

- Any size you would like but at least 2yds long for a long scarf
- Seam allowances are $^1/_4$in. and are included in the cutting size.

Materials

- Silk habotai, silk crêpe de Chine, or silk twill in a length of your choice
- 100 percent cotton thread in ivory—to match the undyed silk
- Natural dye—refer to pages 15–17 for more information on natural dyeing.

Other Tools

- Tape measure
- Fabric scissors
- Sewing machine
- Iron and ironing board
- Pins
- Plastic bucket or container
- Rubber bands
- Rubber gloves

Prepare

Your silk will be $35^1/_2$in.–47in. wide. This is a great width for a scarf. Decide on the length you want the scarf to be and cut a piece 2in. longer than this measurement. This is to allow for hems and natural shrinkage. If you have a rolled hem foot on your sewing machine, hem the scarf on both raw edges. If not, turn and press $^1/_4$in. twice on both raw edges. Pin and then machine- or hand-stitch the edges.
- Go to pages 15–17 to read through the section on natural dyes. Use your leaf, tea, or powdered dye of choice. - Mix up your dye using the relevant fixatives in a plastic bucket. You can start with a small amount of dye and test the color with scraps of silk if you desire. If it's too dark, just add some more boiling water. If it's too light, just add more dye. - Then, choose one of the three patterns and techniques described below.

Pleated Stripes Lay the silk fabric down on a flat surface that is wider than the fabric—a dining table is ideal. - Accordion-fold the fabric from the bottom up, in your desired stripe width—somewhere between $^3/_4$–$1^1/_2$in. You don't need to press these, just keep a good grip on the folds as you go. - Gather a stash of rubber bands (it doesn't matter what color they are). Take your first band and wrap it around one end of the folded fabric. Make sure it is tightly bound. Wrap the second end in the same way so that the folded fabric is stable. Then you can work across the length of the fabric by wrapping a rubber band every $^1/_2$–1in., making sure each band is tight.

Triangle folds Fold the fabric in half lengthwise and press this fold into place. Then fold it in half lengthwise again and press the fold in place. ▣ Lay the silk fabric down on a flat surface that is wider than the fabric. ▣ Fold up the bottom corner of fabric at a 90-degree angle, and then fold it back on itself at a 90-degree angle, creating a triangle shape. Continue to fold backward and forward until you are left with a triangle of fabric. ▣ Bind the fat silk triangle tightly with any number of rubber bands that you want to use. You can crisscross them, or line them horizontally or vertically—or a mixture—just make sure that they are tight.

Circles Lay the fabric on a flat surface that is wider than the fabric. ▣ Decide on a rough design for your scarf—where you want the circles to appear (or be completely random if you'd like to design as you go). ▣ Place marbles, plastic coins, or nonabsorbent circular shapes (raid the toy box!) around your scarf and tie the fabric over the object with a rubber band—make sure this is tied tightly, but be gentle with the silk.

Make

Wearing rubber gloves, immerse the scarf in the dye pot and gently move it around with a spoon. Remove it when the color is slightly darker than you want the scarf to be. Hang up the scarf to dry. This should take about 10–20 minutes. ▣ Rinse the scarf with lukewarm water until the water runs clear. Remove the rubber bands. Hand wash with a mild detergent and warm water, then rinse in cool water. Hang to dry completely, then press lightly if desired.

Design Thoughts

This technique can be used on any natural fabric. Cotton, fine linen, or even wool would be great, but each fabric will take the dye differently and will appear lighter or darker.

You can also use tie-dye to make pillows, throws, or even bed linen. It would make a great contrast to some of the plain dyed linen pillows (see pages 176–178) or against other textiles and patterns.

Antique Silk Scrap Wheat Bags

I'm a hoarder of antique silk fabric. If I've used silk in a quilt or another project I keep all the scraps as they're usually too beautiful to throw away, but also because it feels inherently wrong to throw out something that somebody else has spent so much time and skill making. Sometimes when I'm at markets or fairs I purchase pieces of antique silk samples or damaged textile pieces just because they are fragile and beautiful. I often hand-dye silk velvet for projects and always have small pieces left over. Silk velvet is so tactile that it is perfect for this type of project.

I wanted to use these scraps to make something precious. A quilt would take far too long with so many small pieces, so I thought a wheat bag would be perfect. I've worked out what I think is a very useful and tactile size that's also relatively simple to make.

I've used a combination of silk velvet, kimono silk, a remnant of a fine silk blouse from the 1920s, and lots of little scraps I've had in storage. For something made of what are fundamentally leftovers, there is an innate beauty to these lovely little bags.

Finished Size

- 6in. × 13¾in.
- Seam allowances are ⅜in. and are included in the cutting sizes.

Materials

- You will need scraps of any silk—vintage or new. These can be velvets, brocades, or fine silk linings. You need to be able to cut pieces into one of three sizes: 2¾in. × 2¾in., 6¾in. × 1¾in., or 4¾in. × 2¾in.
- 100 percent cotton thread in a neutral color
- A piece of cotton fabric 15¾in. × 15¾in. for the lining
- A piece of fabric 14½in. × 6¾in. for the backing. This can be silk, cotton, or velvet. I have used a mixture of obi silk and vintage bark cloth.
- Buckwheat hulls
- Dried lavender (optional)

Other Tools

- Iron and ironing board
- Ruler
- Tailor's chalk or dressmaker's pencil
- Rotary cutter and cutting mat (optional)
- Fabric scissors
- Sewing machine with a fine sewing needle and a walking foot attachment
- Pins for delicate fabric
- Kitchen funnel

Prepare

Gently hand wash any of the silk that may need cleaning. Often, vintage pieces may have spots or dust marks. These can be easily removed with delicate laundry liquid. Rinse and dry flat, then gently press.

Cut

For your lining, measure, mark, and cut two pieces that are 14½in. × 6¾in. ▣ For your backing, measure, mark and cut one piece that is 14½in. × 6¾in. ▣ For your front you have three sizes to choose from, which you can mix and match as you please. Look at the pattern and the photos to see different compositions. Depending on the scraps you have, you can choose what to cut and which to put where. I like a mixture of all three sizes. ▣ Measure, mark, and cut out your chosen sizes, then place them in the order you like. Take your time and move them around until you find a composition that works. You can use a rotary cutter and cutting mat to cut out your pieces, but if you don't have these, just use a ruler and dressmaker's pencil to measure the correct sizes before cutting out.

Sew the Inner

Make sure your sewing machine has the walking foot attached and a sewing needle for fine fabrics fitted. Pin your two lining pieces together, right sides facing. Stitch around all four sides, leaving a 4in. gap on one of the longer sides. Press the seams and clip the corners. ▣ Turn the lining right side out and press again. Insert the narrow end of the kitchen funnel into the gap and pour in the buckwheat hulls (and lavender, if you're using it). Try not to overfill as you don't want the wheat bag to be too firm. Gently remove the funnel and pin the open edges together. Slip-stitch closed.

Sew the Outer

First sew the vertical rows together. For example, if you have three of the 2¾in. × 2¾in. squares forming a row, sew these three together. Make sure you have the rights sides facing and do pin first, as silk can move when you are sewing. Gently press the seams open. Repeat as necessary and do the same for any rows in which you have used a square and one of the 4¾in. × 2¾in. rectangles. ▣ Pin each strip together, right sides facing, and sew until you have sewn together the completed front of your wheat bag. ▣ Gently press the seams open.

Complete the Wheat Bag

Pin the wheat bag front to the back. Stitch around all four sides, leaving a 6in. gap on one of the long edges. Press the seams and clip the corners. ▣ Turn the bag outer right side out and gently press again. ▣ Insert the wheat bag inner inside the silk outer. Pin the open seams together and slip-stitch closed.

Design Thoughts

This project is great for building confidence in choosing and marrying fabrics. Deciding what goes with what is often the hardest thing to become comfortable with, so small scale is a great place to start.

This project lends itself to hand sewing or embellishing. I used antique gold thread to stitch the bags closed, but you could also appliqué or embroider them.

You can make the bags longer by adding extra strips, or you can make a 13¾in. square by joining two completed fronts together. Just remember to adjust the size of your inner pieces and your backing.

Tea-Stained Silk Drawstring Bags

I think that precious possessions need precious vessels to contain them. There is something intimate and indulgent about these bags, yet they are so simple to create. Silk habotai has a transformative ability to take a very basic bag shape and turn it into a sensory delight. It is the least expensive of all silks, yet still has that luminosity and tactility that makes these bags very lovely indeed.

By using the natural width of silk habotai (approx. 36in.), you can create three very useful-sized bags—for jewelry, shoes, travel necessities, or maybe just as a holder of special tchotchkes. By dyeing them in a simple tea bath, you add an almost antique feel, which is, I think, exactly what you want from these keepers of loveliness.

Finished Size

- Small $8^{3}/_{4}$in. × $12^{1}/_{4}$in.
- Medium $12^{1}/_{4}$in. × 17in.
- Large $17^{3}/_{4}$in. × 22in.
- Seam allowances are $^{3}/_{8}$in. and are included in the cutting sizes.

Materials

- To make a set of four bags (one large, one medium, and two small) you will need $51^{1}/_{4}$in. silk habotai approx. 36in. wide.
- 100 percent cotton thread in white
- $2^{1}/_{4}$yds silk, silk velvet, or cotton ribbon

Other Tools

- Tape measure
- Iron and ironing board
- Long ruler—at least 24in. long
- Tailor's chalk or dressmaker's pencil
- Fabric scissors
- Pins
- Sewing machine
- Tea bags! I used Earl Grey for a subtle color change.

Cut

Make sure that your piece of silk is exactly $51^{1}/_{4}$in. in length. Fold the width of silk in half and press. Lay the fabric out flat again. Cut one piece $36^{1}/_{4}$in. wide and 24in. long, two pieces 18in. wide and $13^{3}/_{4}$in. long, and one piece $36^{1}/_{4}$in. wide and $13^{3}/_{4}$in. long. Cut along these lines and you will have four pieces of silk. Cut your ribbon into four pieces, each 20in. long.

Sew

Make sure you change your sewing machine needle to one suitable for fine fabrics. You can also use a walking foot to keep the silk from sliding while you are sewing.

For the Large and Small Silk Bags Fold each piece of fabric in half widthwise and pin together. Sew $^{3}/_{8}$in. from the edge along the bottom and the side, stopping $2^{3}/_{4}$in. from the top. Press the seams open and flat. Fold the top edge $^{3}/_{8}$in. to the wrong side and press. Fold over another $^{3}/_{4}$in., press, and pin in place. Sew this seam close to the edge.

For the Medium Silk Bag Follow the same instructions but fold the fabric in half lengthwise to begin with. You will need to sew down two sides rather than a bottom and a side.

Dye

Wash your silk bags and ribbon and squeeze out any excess water. ▫ Get a large pot of water on the stove and bring to a rolling boil. Once the water is boiling, turn off the heat and drop in 3–4 tea bags. Let the tea bags brew for a few minutes and then remove. ▫ Pour in approx. 1 tablespoon of table salt and bring to a boil again. Once the liquid is boiling, reduce the heat to a simmer and drop in your damp silk bags and ribbon, being careful to smooth out any wrinkles. Let them simmer for about 5 minutes and then turn off the heat. ▫ When the water is cool, remove the silk bags and ribbon and wash under a cool tap. Dry flat. ▫ Press your bags and ribbon on a silk setting and pass a ribbon through the top hem of each bag.

Tie the ends of the ribbon together and your delightful tea-stained silk drawstring bags are complete.

Design Thoughts

Experiment with different tea bags. Lots of herbal teas impart beautiful and subtle colors. Regular black tea will give the strongest color. You can always test the color on scraps of silk.

You can, of course, use different fabric for these, but make sure you are using a natural and undyed cloth so that it takes the tea staining as well as it can.

You could use contrasting ribbons rather than dyeing them together. Perhaps you have some antique ribbon that you could use, or cotton lace. You could create a contrast with a metallic or suede drawstring, using scraps left over from one of the leather projects in this book or from haberdashery stores.

Simple Sari Curtain

Curtains can be both difficult and expensive to make. They can also look a bit "done," and that may not be the look you're after. Saris—especially vintage ones—are very beautiful. They come in all sorts of lovely fabrics, such as organza or lightweight silk. The colors and patterns are stunning and the light filters through them beautifully. They are also extremely long, so they're perfect to turn into a simple curtain.

They can work as a lightweight curtain or, to keep you toasty in the winter months, you can also create a separate liner.

Finished Size

Each curtain panel will be approx. 45in. wide with a length of 90–106in. This depends on both the length of the sari and the height of your window. One sari will make two curtain panels

Materials

- Vintage silk sari
- 6yds medium-weight cotton, linen, or wool in a complementary color for the lining. When choosing your lining fabric, take your sari with you and hold the two up to direct light so that you can see how they work together in daylight.
- 100 percent cotton sewing thread

Other Tools

- Curtain pole rod, ends, and bracket
- Curtain rings with integrated clip hooks or separate rings and hooks
- Tape measure
- Tailor's chalk or dressmaker's pencil
- Fabric scissors
- Iron and ironing board
- Pins and a fine-tipped needle
- Sewing machine (optional)

Sari Curtain Panels

Cut

One sari will make a pair of curtains suitable for either a single window or a door. Fold your sari in half lengthwise, press along the fold, and cut along this fold line. You now have two panels. NOTE The top and side edges of the sari panels will already be finished. You will only need to sew the bottom edges.

Measure

These simple curtains shouldn't require too fervently careful a measure as they are meant to be simple. It's fine if they pool slightly or even puddle quite heavily, but it's up to you how much pooling or puddling you're prepared to live with. First decide where your curtain rod will sit on or above your window and install it following the supplier's instructions. Slide the curtain rings and hooks onto the rod—the hook is your measuring point. Measure from the hook to the floor. Add ¾in. to this measurement to allow finishing the cut edge of the sari. Transfer this measurement to the sari panel. If the sari panels are too long, you can trim to size or leave as they are.

Sew

Turn up ⅜in. of the cut edge of the sari and press (make sure your iron is on a low setting for silk). Turn up another ⅜in. and press again. Pin in place and slip-stitch closed.

Your sari curtain panels are complete.

Curtain Liners

Measure

Measure your finished sari panels. ▢ Add 1½in. to the width and 1½in. to the length to get the cutting size of your curtain liners.

Cut

Cut out two panels of fabric to the required measurement.

Sew

Fold over ⅜in. on each side of one panel. Press. Fold over another ⅜in., press, and pin in place. ▢ Either hand- or machine-stitch this seam, close to the edge of the fold mark. ▢ Repeat this for the bottom edge. ▢ For the top edge, fold over ⅜in. and press. Then fold over ¾in., press, and pin into place. Hand- or machine-stitch as your other seams. Your lining panel will be ⅜in. shorter than your sari panel. ▢ One panel is now complete. Repeat for the second lining panel.

Finish

With wrong sides facing together, edge to edge, clip the top edge of both panels in place with the curtain rod clips.

Repeat for your second lining panel, and your delightful sari curtains are complete.

Design Thoughts

If your windows or doors are wider than a one-sari solution, then you could mix and match more than one sari or create a patchwork effect by cutting and sewing pieces together.

You could also have several linings—perhaps a lightweight linen for summer and a dense wool for winter. Or you could use the linings to create different color contrasts—one vivid and one in more subtle tones to change the mood of the room.

Silk Talismans

Talisman is a word derived from *Tilasm*—an Arabic word meaning charm. All over the world, and right back to our earliest history, people have believed that talismans attracted good fortune—that these small and delicate offerings were imbued with magical powers. Talismans are sometimes called amulets and, though these often have a religious overtone, I think the idea of wishing someone well or good fortune is the most important idea behind making them. You might know someone who is having a difficult time, or starting a new adventure, and this would be an incredibly thoughtful gift.

The idea behind this shape is from the Mexican tradition of making heart-shaped amulets or *milagros,* which are then wrapped and placed inside their own container as an individual gift. I wanted to use vintage silk scarves and silk velvet remnants, as these are two of my favorite fabrics, both visually and because of how they feel. These scraps become precious when you give them your time and a little adornment.

Finished size

Approx. 3in. × 3in.

Materials

- Scraps of silk and silk velvet a minimum of 4in. square for the talismans
- Scraps of fabric or leather at least 4¾in. × 4¾in. and 4¾in. × 6in. for the containers
- Silk embroidery thread in a color or colors of your choice
- Filling of your choice—you can use wool, fabric scraps, wheat grains, lavender, or buckwheat hulls
- Any beads, buttons, or sequins for embellishments

Other Tools

- Tailor's chalk or dressmaker's pencil
- Cardboard
- Fabric scissors
- Ruler
- Pins for fine fabric
- Embroidery needle
- Pinking shears

Prepare

Trace the pattern piece at the back of the book onto a firm piece of cardboard.

Cut

For the hearts, cut out as many hearts as you would like to make into talismans. You need two hearts per talisman. For the containers, cut one square 4¾in. × 4¾in. and one rectangle 4¾in. × 6in.

Sew

Pin each pair of hearts together. Hand sew a fine blanket stitch all around the outside, leaving an approx. ¾in. gap on one long side. Leave the needle threaded. Fill the hearts with the filling of your choice, being careful not to overfill. Close the gap by completing the blanket stitch. Tie off, knot, and trim the thread. You can embellish one or both sides of the heart or leave plain. Pin your two container pieces together with the square placed at the bottom of the rectangle. Sew around three sides with right sides out, with a ⅜in. seam allowance. You will have created an envelope. Trim the seams down to approx. ¼in. using pinking shears.

Design Thoughts

You can use traditional boxes instead of a fabric container. These amulets often had a personal message or wish placed inside the heart. This would be lovely if the gift is for a specific reason. You can make these out of any fabric and use any type and color of thread. They can, of course, be used for any occasion—something deeply personal for one person, or for a celebratory gathering of fifty.

Political Freedom Through Weaving Cloth

Swaraj (self-rule) without swadeshi (goods produced within the country) is a lifeless corpse and if swadeshi is the soul of swaraj, khadi is the essence of swadeshi. Therefore khadi became not only a symbol of revolution and resistance but part of an Indian identity.

MAHATMA GANDHI

In India, khadi is not just a cloth—it became a whole movement. India's economy had been failing due to controlled textile imports, effectively shutting down whole villages—not just the weavers, but the blacksmiths, the dyers, and all other supporting small businesses. These villages suffered extreme poverty and a vital loss of cultural identity. Gandhi revitalized the business of weaving, encouraging every man, woman, and child to make cloth   not just to earn money, but to rebuild their communities on every level.

He elevated the physicality of a fabric to become a symbol of strength and self-sufficiency, as well as providing employment for millions of people during India's struggle for freedom. That extraordinary symbolism of wearing cloth made by human hands continues to this day.

127 HIDE

Ooohh, leather

—it is the stuff of expensive shoes and bags, as well as antique chairs and wee notebooks. Most of us love it—some of us don't. Fred and Wilma Flintstone were cloaked in it, and we always ask "Is it leather?" when eyeing up a new purchase. It is also the textile we financially invest in most.

I still remember the (very expensive) suede jacket I bought when I was 22 years old. I was off on my global adventures and felt I needed something to mark the occasion, as well as to shield me from any potential difficulties. I wish I still had it, because it certainly had its share of adventures/catastrophes. I'm sure there are thousands of leather jackets out there with excellent stories to share if they could.

We are sad when a favorite pair of shoes wears out, and we hanker for beautiful bags. Some of us don't like to use leather or any form of hide—and that's absolutely fine. Every project here can be made with another type of cloth.

It is, of course, the most ancient of all fibers—man was wrapping himself in it long before he discovered weaving or felting. It was primal in the truest sense. Babies still love sheepskins, and aging leather chairs are the most comfortable. Not only is leather tactile, but it is also very protective. A leather jacket only gets better with age and shelters us from knocks and falls, as well as the elements. Leather shoes and bags can be mended instead of thrown away. As with all natural cloths, there is good and bad—and compromise in between. As much as I am keen on mindful making, I believe conscious consumption is as important. If you don't know the complicated manufacturing methods, then you don't know what options there are, but hopefully the following will help you understand and make slightly more educated choices.

Prehistoric man used leather for almost everything—holding water, bags, harnesses, shelter, and footwear. Before he realized how to shear the sheep, he wore their skins on his back. Man somehow discovered a way to preserve skins by using smoke, grease, and bark extracts. Wall paintings and artifacts found in Egyptian tombs circa 1,300 BC show that leather was used for sandals, clothes, buckets, bottles, and shrouds for burying the dead. Greeks were using leather around 1,200 BC. The Romans used leather for almost everything—footwear, clothes and shields, saddles and harnesses for military warfare. Large quantities of leather clothing and footwear have been found in England in excavated Roman sites. The main armor of the Roman soldier was a heavy leather shirt, and leather goods were often prized as much as jewelry.

Most countries developed their own technique of turning skins into leather and the process was kept a closely guarded secret, passed down from father to son. Through the centuries leather manufacturing grew. In medieval times most towns and villages had a tannery, on the edge of town by a stream or river. Although necessary, tanning was considered an "odoriferous trade," as the smell was so invasive. Wandering through the souks of Marrakech today provides an olfactory reminder of how this would have smelled.

Leather is created by tanning animal rawhide and skin. The majority of leather comes from cows, although many other animal skins can be tanned. It can be manufactured in large plants or small cottage industries. There are many ways in which the skins can be tanned—some are better than others due to their methods, use of natural resources, treatment of humans and animals, and lack of harmful chemical process. Vegetable tanning was the main technique used until the 19th century as the materials needed were widely available and chemical methods had not yet been created. As new methods were researched, vegetable tanning was supplemented by chrome tanning. Once leather has been tanned, there are different types of finishes, which are usually reflected in the price of the skin and finished goods. Leather used for pieces sold in a store on Rodeo Drive is likely to be a far superior quality and finish than the leather in your local mall.

Full-grain hides have not been sanded or buffed to remove imperfections. The skin breathes and wears better, developing a patina rather than wearing out. It is the highest-quality leather available.

Top-grain leather is second best. It has had a split layer removed and the skin is sanded and coated to avoid staining. It doesn't breathe as well and feels colder to the touch due to its coating.

Corrected leather has an artificial grain applied to its surface. It's usually made from lower-grade skins that come from marked or torn hides and ends up as colored skins so that the flaws aren't obvious.

Split leather is the leftover from top-grain leather. Split leather can be separated into many layers until it is too fine to split any further. It can have an artificial layer applied and embossed to look like leather grain. It's also used for suede.

Of course, leather isn't for everyone. It will often depend on how you feel about meat. Many people will wear leather based on the notion that it is a by-product of meat. Sometimes it is, but sometimes it isn't. Of course, you can then weigh in with organic or free-range skins compared to intensively farmed skins. So first you have to decide if you want to use leather, then what tanning process is acceptable to you, and, finally, which original source. All this is complicated but, hopefully, thought-provoking.

You can, of course, use many other fabrics in place of leather. There are now pseudo-leather materials available, such as vegan microfiber, pleather, or nu-suede. These are all man-made materials, so if you don't like the idea of those, you can use wool, wool felt, waxed canvas, or any other sturdy natural cloth that suits you.

Production

Creating leather is a lengthy and complicated process. The use of chemicals and how they are disposed of is a constant problem, although there are continual improvements in the type and quantity of chemicals used. Each country has different environmental regulations and, unfortunately, some of them are not very robust—leading to significant water and air pollution. Finding out where your leather came from and how it was tanned is a good start to choosing skins.

The variants are never-ending, so this is very much the short version—a version without graphic details. To turn hides into leather, they need to be prepped, tanned, and crusted.

The prepping starts with curing the hides in salt. They are then soaked, limed, dehaired, delimed, drenched, and, if necessary, pickled and depickled. . . This is just to get the hide ready for tanning.

Tanning is where it all starts to get a bit complicated. Tanning makes the hide flexible and stable—that's the easy part. The not so easy and hotly contested part is how it is tanned. The process of tanning leather can be incredibly toxic. Most leather is chrome-tanned, which results in carcinogenic waste being pumped into water reserves. Most of Europe and the United States no longer use chromium to tan leather, but the rest of the world still does. Unfortunately, chrome tanning is faster and produces more flexible leather than nontoxic vegetable tanning. It all comes down to a matter of conscience, really.

Vegetable-tanned leather is exactly that. The process uses tannin and tree bark to create the color, and no chemicals. Vegetable-tanned leather does tend to discolor and doesn't react well to being left in water, but it is becoming more popular again due to its production method. The leather can also be oiled to repel water. Chrome-tanned leather processed using chromium sulfate and formaldehyde is now being phased out, as it is simply dangerous for people to work with. Rose-tanned leather uses pure rose otto oil to tan the hides—the most expensive method of tanning there is. Leather can also be tanned using synthetic polymers. Last—for the cowboys among you—is rawhide. Rawhide is simply scraped, soaked, and stretched leather that is used for drumheads, cords, and dog chews.

Once the hide is prepped and tanned, it needs to be crusted. Crusting is the process by which the hide is thinned, lubricated, and finished. Any buffing, waxing, dyeing, spraying, embossing, or polishing happens at this point.

When you buy leather, it is usually priced by the square foot and sold as a complete hide, not as a square. Sometimes larger hides are precut into smaller pieces, or you can purchase offcuts. Skins from smaller animal are sold whole.

Many other skins can and have been processed into leather or "fur-on" hides. Here are a few:

Lambskin is used as soft leather for expensive clothing, and sheepskins are used in our homes and to cosset our babies. Pigskin is also used in apparel and on the seats of saddles.

Deerskin is a tough but smooth leather and is mostly used for coats, or for wallets and bags. Most deerskin is no longer procured from the wild, with deer farms breeding the animals specifically for the purpose of their skins. Elk skin is also available, and is used for shoes, work gloves, and dog collars.

Many fish can be used to produce leather. *Salmon skin* has fine scales and is strong. It is farmed in Norway and Iceland. *Perch* is farmed in Egypt and is recognized by its large, round, and soft scales. *Shagreen*, or stingray, is an incredibly expensive leather and is mostly used for furniture.

Kangaroo skin is used to make goods that need to be strong and flexible—motorcycle jackets, falconry equipment, and football shoes, to name a few.

Originally grown for its feathers, the ostrich is now farmed predominantly for its meat and its leather. *Ostrich leather* is now used across all high-end products—bags, shoes, upholstery, and inside luxury cars. It has a "goose bump" look because of the large follicles from which the feathers grow.

Metallic Leather Sling

I love metallic leather—well, metallic anything, to be honest. There is a wonderful contrast in texture and light that metallic goods provide against other surfaces. Metallic surfaces pick up and mirror light and these reflections can make you and your home feel good—it seems to have the same effect as a little sparkle or glitter. Many types of cloth can be metallicized through dyeing, spraying, painting, or printing, and I think it works particularly well on leather. Bags, shoes, and purses always look great when they are silver, pewter, or gold, and they work as well with jeans and a T-shirt as they do with the ubiquitous little black dress.

You may think this bag sounds impossible to source and make—it was, in fact, one of the easiest projects in this book. Lambskin suppliers are not difficult to find and lambskin is thin enough to sew on a domestic sewing machine. The bag is built on a very simple construction method, which I think works really well for metallic material, and there are only five seams involved in total (and a little bit of topstitching).

Finished Size

- 17¾in. (w) × 23¼in. (h)
- Seam allowances are ⅜in. and are included in the pattern pieces.

Materials

- A piece or several pieces of lambskin. I bought a whole lambskin and had plenty left over but, whichever supplier you purchase from, if you explain your size needs they are usually very happy to help (leather people are always really helpful, I find).
- 100 percent cotton thread in a color to match your piece of leather. You can use metallic thread, but as long as it is tonally matching you should be fine.

Other Tools

- Pins
- Tailor's chalk or dressmaker's pencil
- Fabric scissors
- Leather needle for your sewing machine
- Sewing machine with walking foot attachment

Prepare

Cut out or trace the sling pattern in the back of the book. ▫ Check your piece of leather for any blemishes and mark out the best position for your pattern pieces. You will have some waste but you can always use this to make zippered purses, pillows, or many of the other projects in this book.

Cut

Using weights or pins, secure the pattern piece to the lambskin. Trace around the pattern piece and, using very sharp scissors, cut out four of the sling body. Make sure you cut two with the pattern facing right-side up and two with the pattern laid down with the right side facing down.

It's important to use a walking foot when sewing leather together, as it will keep it from sliding or catching. Change the needle to a leather needle on your sewing machine.

▫ Pin two of the sling pieces together at side A, right sides facing, and sew the seam together. Finger press the seams open and topstitch along each side of the join, making sure you keep the leather open and flat on the wrong side. Join the two handles together in the same way and topstitch again. ▫ Repeat for the remaining two pieces.

▫ Pin the two sides together with right sides facing. Sew around the two sides and the bottom. Clip the corners and finger press the seams open.

Turn your bag right side out, and you're done.

Design Thoughts

This bag is such a great shape—it can be casual or smart, day or evening and, as the pattern is so simple, it is both quick and cost-effective to make.

You can use any leather you like as long as it is thin enough to go through your homesewing machine. If the leather is slightly on the thicker side, you may find it difficult to topstitch, but you don't have to do that step anyway. Any leather that is listed as clothing weight is usually great for this bag.

If you want to use thicker leather, you could always get a shoe repair shop or a local machinist to make it up for you (that may be defeating the object of making but if you've found the leather and cut the pattern out, you're definitely a maker).

If you don't want to use leather, the sling also works well with waxed canvas or sailing canvas, as it doesn't unravel. If you wanted to use a denim, upholstery-weight linen or canvas, you just need to stitch $^3/_8$in. from the edge, around the opening edge and handles. You can also make contrast lining and stitch this together in the same way.

Once you have made one bag, why not adjust the pattern to make a different style? You can lengthen the body and create a gusset bottom (see the Canvas Market Tote on pages 26–29 for instructions). Or you could lengthen the straps so that it can sit across your body rather than on your shoulder. You can also remove the center join if you're using fabric rather than leather. You can also add a pocket or pockets on the inside or outside of the bag. Last, but not least, you could shrink it down to make a smaller handbag version, with or without a gusset and pockets. Phew. . . Oh—and if you have any leather left over you could use it to make some of the zippered purses, hand-stitched purses, or journal in this book on pages 42–45, 138–139, or 142–145.

Natural Leather Purses

You can buy leather in just about any color or finish you like. However, you can also buy it simply vegetable tanned, with no other treatment. The leather starts off a kind of muted flesh tone but then ages and darkens over time to this wonderful light chestnut color—a color that can't be replicated, it seems, by any commercial dyes. I like how being handled by human hands changes something very naturally beautiful into a chronology of personal use.

Finished Size

There are three patterns available, all based on an envelope or simple container shape:

- Small — $3\frac{3}{4}$in. × 5in.
- Medium — 5in. × 7in.
- Large — 7in. × $10\frac{1}{4}$in.

Materials

- You will need a piece of undyed vegetable-tanned leather to fit the number of purses you would like to make. The thickness needs to be at least $\frac{1}{32}$in.—and up to $\frac{1}{8}$in.

Other Tools

- Stiff cardboard
- Dressmaker's pencil or pen
- Very sharp scissors or utility knife and cutting mat
- 1 button and washer screw fitting per purse
- Awl or leather hole punch

Prepare

Trace or cut out the purse patterns provided in the back of the book. Trace these onto stiff cardboard, transferring the markings for the button placement.

Cut

All leather has marks and imperfections. Check your leather to find a good position to transfer your patterns to. Using weights to keep the pattern secure, trace around the edges of the pattern pieces, then cut out using either very sharp scissors or a utility knife.

Make

The making is very simple indeed. Transfer the points for the button and washer and make the correct-sized hole using either an awl or a leather hole punch. Fit the button and washer using fitting tools and you're done.

- Or, make another one or three.

Design Thoughts

It goes without saying that you can use any leather you like for this project, but it does need to be reasonably firm. The button washers are available in a variety of finishes so you can change the look and feel from modern and utilitarian to something very vintage.

You can paint leather—it's a natural surface so will take paint well. Rustle up a landscape or write a story or even just a message of giving.

And you can change the size. Use a photocopier to enlarge or reduce the patterns—the larger the finished purse is, the firmer the leather will need to be.

Sheepskin-Covered Stool

Natural fibers thrill our fingertips. Using our sense of touch is vital to our well-being and touch thrives on contrast and variety. Sheepskins offer an irresistible opportunity for tactile indulgence. I believe that the positive feelings we get from sheepskins or any fur are primeval. They offer more emotional warmth and comfort than any other fiber group, and we respond to them at a very simple level—they feel good, so we do, too.

We had a stool like this when I was growing up and I loved it. It was always in my mother's room and I can remember sitting on it with my fingers firmly rooted in its fur and legs swinging. As a project, it is a little nostalgic for me, but I also think it's a wondrous piece of furniture for big and small people to rest on and enjoy.

Finished Size

Any size you like

Materials

- ▣ An upholstered stool of your choice—this can be antique, vintage, or new
- ▣ Sheepskin—make sure it's large enough to cover the top and sides of your stool, with extra to fix to the underside

Other Tools

- ▣ Staple gun (electric is great if you have one)
- ▣ Sharp scissors

Prepare

Decide if you need to modify or improve the stool in any way—whether by painting, sanding, stripping, or waxing. You need to do this before you attach the sheepskin. ▣ If you are using an antique or vintage piece, you also need to decide if you want to remove the old upholstery. Perfectionists would say yes, but you may not like what you find underneath. . . which means you'll have to replace the upholstery as well. It's up to you whether you want this to be a short or a long project.

Make

If your stool has removable legs, remove these now. Lay the sheepskin right side down and center the stool on top. Pull the edges of the sheepskin over it and staple them down onto the wooden frame of the stool. Make sure you pull the sheepskin tight as you go and fold the corners in. ▣ Trim away any excess so that you have a nice clean line. Reattach the stool legs, if necessary, and you're done—except for finding a good place in your home for it to sit.

Design Thoughts

I've made this a very simple project, but you can make it more "professional" by ensuring the stool is freshly upholstered, if necessary, and applying a lining to the underside of the stool.

There is a wide variety of sheepskins available now. As farmers are introducing rare breeds back into their flocks, so their skins become accessible. They are usually wonderful colors and more natural in appearance than many of the commercial skins. It's worth spending a little time and a little more money supporting an artisan business in which you know the herd has had a good life and the animals have been treated humanely.

Leather Journal

I have piles of journals of every shape and size around my studio. I love them for their look and the feel of the unmarked paper. But most of all, I love what they promise—there's a world waiting to be created inside every one of them—you just have to dream it up.

Sometimes, you need a large book for design and drawing or a little notebook to keep in your bag for "life-lists." Or you might want a travel journal big enough to keep together all those postcards and bits of ephemera you've picked up on your adventures. A new journal is always exciting; a full one, incredibly satisfying.

Books are easy to make—they've been made by hand for centuries. The addition of soft leather covers makes them wonderfully tactile, but also a little more long-lasting while you fill their pages with doodles, dreams, lists, or opera tickets.

Finished Size

To match your chosen paper, up to letter (8½" x 11") size

Materials

- Sheets of paper of different weights, colors, or types. You can mix graph paper with wax paper, cotton paper with fine onion-skin paper, patterned paper with watercolor paper—any paper at all. The paper will need to be twice the size of the finished journal (when folded in half widthwise).
- A piece of lambskin, goatskin, or book-binding leather in a color of your choice
- Embroidery thread in a color of your choice

Other Tools

- Long ruler—at least 24in. long
- Pencil
- Utility knife and cutting mat
- Old blanket or towel
- Awl
- Large upholstery or tapestry needle

Plan

Decide on the size of your journal and cut any paper to size, if necessary. Place the paper sheets on top of each other in an order that you like. You can build up to a thickness of approx. ¼in. The thicker the paper stack is, the larger you'll need to make the leather outer.

Complete the Paper Inner

Press each sheet of paper in half and crease the fold line. Lay back down opened. Repeat for every piece of paper and rebuild your stack. Doing this will make the book fold nicely and give you an easy position to punch the holes.

Prepare the Leather Cover

Measure the thickness of your folded paper. On the underside of the leather, draw a rectangle that is the same height as the stack of folded paper and the same length as the paper stack plus the thickness of the folded paper. This allows the leather cover to wrap around the whole book without exposing the edges of the paper. Using your utility knife and ruler, carefully cut out the rectangle.

Finishing the Journal

Put the leather cover open, outer side down, and place the pages inside.▢ Using your awl, punch 8–12 holes evenly through the center of the spine.▢ Cut a piece of embroidery thread at least four times the height of the book. Thread the needle and begin by sewing from inside the pages and cover to the outside, starting from the top hole. Weave in and out, tightening as you go, until the book feels secure. Finish on the inside of the book, tighten, and tie off. You can either leave the excess thread to act as a bookmark, or trim it away.

Your journal is complete.

Design Thoughts

These journals can be incredibly minimalist or be stuffed full of different kinds of paper—translucent, patterned, lined, watercolor, or beautiful handmade paper. You can look around in art or stationery stores as well as specialist paper stores (what a way to while away an afternoon!). The paper can be new or old—perhaps old notepaper that belonged to your grandmother, or embossed paper secreted away from a special hotel. Mix and match—tell a story with the paper that you will fill with actual stories and lists.

It can be useful to include envelopes in your journal as they are incredibly handy for ticket stubs and scraps of precious cloth. Just puncture them through the top crease of the envelope so that they can close again.

Another idea is to preprint your paper with lines or headings, quotes, or poems so that these feature throughout the book.

The more paper you add, the wider you need the leather to be, so that it can encase the insides. You can also make your journal more robust by increasing the width of the leather cover to create flaps. When you fold the book in half, you can fold the extra leather in to protect the edges of the paper.

You can use any leather for the outer—from fine glove leather to robust saddlery leather. The thicker the leather, the more patient you'll need to be when cutting and hole punching. Alternatively, you can pop along to your local shoe repairer and get them to cut and punch for you.

If you don't want to use leather, the journal would also work with any strong fabric such as moleskin, felt, or even card.

Instead of embroidery silk, you could use linen thread (always used in leathercraft), wool, or even a fine ribbon.

Suede Drawstring Pouch

When you visit antique shows or textile fairs, suede goods pop up on the most glamorous of stalls. I have found pairs of vintage suede driving gloves and jewelry boxes lined in tobacco-colored suede. Suede blouson jackets from the 1930s are incredibly alluring—and my very favorite interiors book has a suede cover, too (it's beside me as I write). Suede is more subtle than leather and, because it is so fine, it's perfect to sew with at home—which is very useful if you're wanting to add a little glamour to your life.

Finished Size

- 9½in. × 11½in.
- Seam allowances are ⅜in. and are included in the pattern pieces.

Materials

- A piece of lamb-, sheep-, or goatskin suede at least 24in. × 31½in. Skins won't come in a rectangular shape like fabric, but you can buy it by the square foot, or a half or whole skin. The suede can be any color that takes your fancy but needs to be about ¹⁄₃₂–¹⁄₁₆in. thick in order to sew it on a domestic sewing machine.
- 100 percent cotton thread in a matching color

Other Tools

- Tailor's chalk or dressmaker's pencil
- Pins
- Fabric scissors
- Leather needle for your sewing machine
- Sewing machine with walking foot attachment
- Hole punch, leather punch, or awl

Prepare

Cut out or trace the pouch pattern provided at the back of the book. ▫ Check your piece of suede for any blemishes and mark out the best position for your pattern pieces.

Cut

Using pins, secure the pattern pieces to the suede. Trace around the pattern piece and, using very sharp scissors, cut out two of the pouch body and two of the drawstrings.
- Use the pattern piece to mark your drawstring holes on each piece of suede.

Sew

It's important to use a walking foot when sewing leather together as it will keep it from moving or catching. Change the needle on your sewing machine to a leather needle.
▫ Pin the pouch together, right sides facing, and sew around the two sides and bottom. Clip the corners and finger press the seams open. ▫ Turn the pouch right side out. Using either your hole or leather punch, make the holes as marked. You can always practice on some scrap suede first to get the hang of creating holes. ▫ Thread one drawstring through each side and tie the ends together.

Design Thoughts

You can use any soft leather for these pouches—deerskin is particularly lovely to sew with, or you could try lambskin.

You can scale the size of the pouch up or down simply by enlarging or reducing the pattern on a photocopier. You could make a group of these pouches to hold jewelry or as a really beautiful wrapping for a special present.

Blue Gold

Indigo is a blue pigment extracted from the leaves of indigo-producing plants. There are several kinds but the most common is Indigofera, which grows in India, Africa, Asia, the Middle East, and all of the Americas. Unlike other natural dyes, because of its unique chemistry indigo is compatible with all natural fibers—whether from animals or vegetables—which means they all absorb the color superbly. The dye itself is green and it is only when the cloth is pulled out of the vat that the true blue is revealed. Every dip in the dye produces a darker shade, so skilled dyers can create a whole palette of blues.

Indigo is one of the world's oldest and most valued dyes and remains one of the last natural dyes to be used instead of synthetics. Developing nations such as Benin and Guatemala still hand-dye with indigo and the rivers still run blue. It does require skill to dye with indigo (and it does smell), but you can easily take a one-day course—just be prepared to be in love with indigo at the end of it.

Indigo plants grow in most corners of the globe—temperate or tropical. Indigo runs as a refrain through cultures and countries. It is probably also the dye we love most—from our jeans to shibori kimonos, it remains incredibly stylish and sought-after.

Below is a short reference list of indigo people, places, and goods:

England—William Morris, or Blue Topsy as his friends called him, was the indigo master. It took him eight years to master indigo dyeing, but his indigo vats remained in use until his company closed in 1940.

France—The French tended to use woad, which dyes a lighter blue, instead. You can find indigo in sheets and peasant smocks.

Bali—Wonderful Ikat.

Chile—Ikat ponchos and horse blankets—lucky horse!

Italy—The Romans used indigo as a pigment for painting and for medicinal and cosmetic purposes.

South Africa—The marvelous Shweshwe cloth.

Japan—Indigo is the traditional color for the yukata summer kimono, as this clothing recalls nature and the blue sea. It is also the color of the incredible Japanese boro—rags or bedding that are continually patched to show the history of the maker. At the finer end of the fabric spectrum are their shibori cloths—my absolute favorite.

United States—Blue jeans and blue-collar shirts helped create the country's cultural identity.

Laos—The Lanten women of the Luang Namtha Valley are the key—a large community of women who still hand-dye cloth for their community and others.

China—Known for hand-drawn batik from the Miao Hmong women.

Vietnam—The Black Hmong women of Sa Pa dyed all of their clothing a deep, deep blue.

Ghana—The incredible wax prints—another favorite.

Benin—The men tie-dye indigo cotton of exceptional quality.

Sumatra—Karo batak dyers include blood to make their cloth dark and shiny.

Niger and Nigeria—Haoussa Muslims weave Ikat-dyed indigo cloth.

Mali—Tritik shibori—stunning.

India—Block-printed cotton, resist-printed and bandhini cloth. Dyers are generally Muslim, as Hindus regard dyeing as an impure occupation due to the processes used.

151

LINEN

We slumber under it for a blissful sleep and wear it on carefree summer days. We stalk antique shows for perfect embroidered sheets and daub our personal masterpieces on its canvas. Linen can be so fine it is almost transparent, or chunky and crunchy.

Linen is the oldest textile plant cultivated in Europe and is so much a part of our history that it is referred to as the "fiber of civilization." When starched, it is indeed civilized as fine dining napkins but, thickly woven, it is outstanding and extremely comforting as upholstery.

To be a spinster was no bad thing in the 17th century—it simply meant an unmarried woman who was busy weaving this wonderful cloth. If only it meant that now...

Linen is made from the stem of the flax plant, which grows anywhere the climate is temperate and moist. Its botanical name, *Linum usitatissimum*, means "extremely useful"—and useful it is. It is healthy and beneficial for the skin as it keeps you warm in winter and cool in summer. It's nonallergenic and antibacterial, which means it's good for us.

This fabric is also very good for our planet. Flax needs five times less fertilizers and pesticides to grow than cotton and—just like very good wine—it needs no irrigation. Turning flax into linen can be respectful to the environment, as it is purely mechanical, using neither solvents nor water. Spinning linen can be difficult, though, as its fibers are smooth and they need a damp atmosphere and human hands to stick together.

Linen is a very durable, strong fabric and is stronger when wet than dry. Linen has been used for sails, fishing nets, and fire hoses, as the fibers do not stretch and they resist abrasion. When properly manufactured, linen has the ability to absorb and lose water rapidly. It can gain up to 20 percent moisture without feeling damp—ideal for a tropical holiday ensemble.

Mildew, perspiration, and bleach can damage linen, but it is resistant to moths and carpet beetles. It also resists dirt and stains, has no lint or pilling tendency, and can be dry-cleaned, machine-washed, or steamed. Every time linen is washed, a subtle molecular change takes place around each fiber, so it comes up looking like new. It withstands high temperatures, too, and has only minimal initial shrinkage. So far, so good, but there is even more.

It has a wonderful crisp and textured feel to it and feels cool to touch. Linen thread can be spun into a variety of thicknesses, historically ranging from workaday shepherds' smocks to the very fine undergarments of the gentry. It can vary from stiff and rough to delicate and smooth.

Linen has a wonderful luster, with natural colors in shades of ivory, ecru, or gray, whereas pure white linen is created through bleaching. Although linen can be dyed, it doesn't accept most natural dyes very well (however, indigo and woad are perfect for linen), unlike animal-derived fibers. It does, however, have the advantage of washing whiter and softer with age and, because the fabric lasts so long, up until the 17th century garments made from linen were historically gifted in wills.

Its place in homes was gradually usurped by cotton, especially during the 19th century, when cotton mills became prevalent and cotton was far cheaper. However, for those who could afford it, linen was still preferred for its fineness, usefulness, and durability.

History

Linen has been a little taken for granted in fabric history—perhaps because its manufacture was so everyday. Families in many countries around the world had their own flax garden. To make linen fabric was just another household chore, like fetching water from the well or killing livestock.

Every family would have tried to grow enough for their own home, with any excess used to pay tithes and taxes owing. Itinerant weavers would travel between villages and homes to make cloth from the spun yarn. By the 17th century, however, the majority of woven linen was imported from France and Belgium.

The earliest written mention of linen comes from ancient Greece, where its production and industry was "written" down on 4,000-year-old tablets. Egyptian mummies were wrapped in linen (each needing an extraordinary 4,000ft^2) because linen was seen as a symbol of light and purity and as a display of wealth. While living, the Egyptians wore only white linen because of the extreme heat—perhaps the historical starter for our own linen-shirt-wearing habits in summer.

When Pharaoh Ramesses II's tomb was discovered in 1881, the linen that had been wrapped around his mummy more than 3,000 years before was perfectly preserved, as were the linen curtains in the tomb of Tutankhamen when it was opened in 1922.

Many verses in the Bible mention linen as a fabric of fineness and beauty, with the angels described as wearing white linen for purity.

Linen was first introduced into Ireland around 900 BC by Phoenecian traders, although some historians believe it could have traveled through the British Isles with the Romans. However it was introduced, it was the Romans who set up linen factories in Ireland to supply clothing for their soldiers.

In the early 12th century, the Brehon laws made it compulsory for farmers to learn and practice the cultivation of flax and manufacture of linen cloth.

Medieval baths were often made of wood and lengths of linen were used to line them for greater comfort. Detachable collars and cuffs were historically made from linen and a beautifully pressed and folded linen pocket-handkerchief was essential to being a well-dressed man during the early 20th century.

Today, flax is grown in many parts of the world but, as with most natural fabrics, bulk linen production has moved to Eastern Europe and China. The highest-quality linen is still created by artisan producers in Ireland, Italy, France, and Belgium. Antique and vintage linen sheets are coveted for their quality, and beautifully made contemporary linen commands a justifiably high price for something that not only feels fantastic, but will also last for a very long time.

Production

Linen has a very long journey from field to cloth. It's also incredibly physically demanding to create. The plant is sown in April, flowers in June, and is harvested in August. Creating cloth from the plant starts with soaking the flax stems (retting), followed by crushing and beating (scutching), and then combing (or heckling). It all sounds a bit brutal, doesn't it?

To get the very best fibers, flax is either hand-harvested by pulling up the entire plant or the stalks are cut very close to the root. The seeds are then removed through a mechanized process called "rippling" or by hand winnowing.

The fibers are then loosened from the stalk through retting. Retting uses bacteria to decompose the pectin that binds the fibers together—it's basically controlled rotting. Natural retting can happen in tanks and pools, or directly in the fields. There are chemical retting methods that are faster, but are obviously more harmful to the environment and to the fibers themselves. In Egypt the stalks are still retted by soaking in the Nile, which must be an extraordinary sight to witness.

After retting, the stalks are ready for scutching. Scutching mechanically crushes the stalks and separates the fibers. Other parts of the stalks, such as linseed, shive, and tow are used for other products. The fibers are then heckled or combed. The short fibers are combed away leaving the lovely long, soft flax fibers behind. This flax is then spun into yarn. Wet spinning makes soft, fine yarn for clothing and dry spinning creates a heavy, chunky yarn.

Uses

Linen cloth has traditionally been regarded as the "workhorse" of fabrics as it can be used to fulfill almost every personal and household need. It can be heavenly sheets (yes please), fine clothing, robust napkins, and upholstery fabric, to name a few uses. It's often used in luggage, as painters' canvas, and even surgical thread. We pack summer linen clothes for holidays and covet antique textiles for our homes. In fact, besides silk, it is the fabric we seem to desire most.

Artisan bakers use linen as a couche to hold dough in shape during its final rise. Simple linen sacks are then used to keep the baked bread fresh—genius.

Irish linen is often used to wrap pool and billiard cues, as it is ruthlessly efficient at absorbing the sweat from the players' hands—slightly unpleasant to think about, but very useful for the players in high-stress situations. Linen also makes very strong and crisp paper: so strong, in fact, that many countries print their currency on paper that is made from a mixture of linen and cotton.

Vintage and antique linens are usually as good (or better) quality than new linen and can be used to create wonderful upholstery and soft furnishings. As well as being very strong, antique cloth is incredibly tactile in handle as well as spirit—after all, you are feeling the hands and history of the makers.

Different but Similar

Hemp is a very fast-growing crop and can produce 250 percent more fiber than cotton and 600 percent more fiber than flax with the same amount of land. It's also good for our land as it adds healthy organic matter to the soil and helps to retain moisture. It is very strong and the most durable of all natural fabrics. Hemp fabric holds its shape and is soft, comfortable, and incredibly durable. It is also naturally resistant to mold and will dye and retain color better than cotton. Just like linen, it is warm in winter and cool in summer. And just like linen, it feels delightful. You can use hemp in place of linen for most homewares, although it will probably be blended with cotton, linen, or silk for clothing.

Linen Slippers

Crossing the threshold from the outside world into a home is a mental as well as physical gesture. Taking off your coat and putting down your bag in a warm and welcoming hallway is one of life's simplest pleasures. Kicking off your shoes is probably the most symbolic gesture. The outside world is somewhere else and you're really home. I'm always happy when guests are content enough to slip off their shoes—it means my home is welcoming and that's a very good feeling.

Staying barefoot at home in high summer is a childlike thrill but, more often than not, you need to wear something and this is where the slipper comes in. Slippers are far simpler to make than you think and take very little fabric, so you can use lovely, tactile cloth. They make wonderful presents for friends and family of all ages and are particularly lovely to give to guests when they arrive after a long journey. I can't think of anything more charming or hospitable—apart from a roaring fire and a delicious meal.

Finished Size

The pattern comes in two sizes:
- Small/medium: up to ladies' size 7½/men's size 5½
- Medium/large: ladies' size 7½–10/men's size 5½–8
- Seam allowances are ⅜in. and are included in the pattern pieces.

Materials

- 22in. fabric will comfortably make you two pairs of slippers, but you can use scraps from other projects. For these slippers, I have used a mixture of nubbly washed artist's canvas, hemp, Japanese indigo linen, and the Belgium linen lining I used for the sari curtains (see pages 118–121).
- 100 percent cotton thread in a neutral color to match your main fabric
- 100 percent cotton thread in a contrasting color of your choice
- 12in. × 12in. piece of batting or fleece per pair of slippers

Other Tools

- Iron and ironing board
- Tailor's chalk or dressmaker's pencil
- Fabric scissors
- Pins
- Sewing machine
- Hand-sewing needle

Prepare

Prewash the fabric on a warm wash to eliminate any shrinkage. Dry, then press with a hot iron. Cut out or trace the two pattern pieces provided in the back of the book. Note that there are two sizes, so make sure that you match the right top to the right bottom.

Cut

Using pins, secure the pattern pieces to your fabric. Trace around them, ensuring you transfer all the markings as well, then cut out four of the bottom and four of the top pieces per pair of slippers. Trace the bottom pattern piece onto your batting or fleece. Cut out two.

Sew

Pin two top pieces right sides together and stitch along line A. Press the curved seams flat and clip if necessary. Turn the right side out and press again. Repeat for the second pair of top pieces. ▫ Change the thread on your sewing machine to the contrasting color. Pin one of the bottom pieces to the batting with the right side facing up, away from the batting. Decoratively stitch the two pieces together. You can choose how many lines, how wide apart they should be and in which direction they should travel. ▫ Change the thread on your sewing machine back to the neutral color. Pin the two bottom pieces and the top piece together, with the top piece sandwiched in the middle and the bottom pieces right sides toward the middle. Match all markings—you will have to curve the top piece to fit. Stitch the three sections together, leaving the gap as marked on your pattern. Press the seams open with a medium to hot iron and trim or clip excess fabric away. Turn the slipper right side out and press again. Slip-stitch the open seam closed.

Repeat for the second slipper, and the pair is complete.

Design Thoughts

The fabric world is your oyster when it comes to slippers, as they are perfect for using up scraps. I've used linen as I wanted a light pair for spring, but I've also made them in wool and leather. Make sure the fabric you use for the bottom is not "slippy," to avoid accidents. Linen in particular has a nubbly texture so you won't slide around on the floor.

Use fabrics that you can wash or wipe clean. You can use just one or four different fabrics per slipper—it's up to you.

You can also choose the color of the contrast stitching to either contrast vividly or blend in subtly. Sew in the direction and with an intensity that works for you.

Last, but not least, if you don't have any batting or fleece available, you can use several layers of wool—it just needs to be thick enough to make the slippers comfortable to wear.

Hessian Curtain Panel or Simple Headboard

Hessian is an often underrated cloth. It is very simple in construction and slightly rough to the touch, but is a very practical natural fabric to use. It is usually woven from the skin of the jute plant or from sisal fibers.

Historically found as coffee sacks, military clothing, in the building trade, or as the "undergarment" in upholstery, more recently hessian has been used in a more refined finish for fashion, home furnishings, and "eco" goods.

It is great for bags or, filled, as floor pillows, but I thought it would also be perfect to use as a simple curtain panel or headboard. As a fabric, hessian is incredibly economical and it lets in light but also provides screening from whatever it is you don't want to see. As a curtain, it can't be drawn, but can be used in a room, studio, or office in which you need permanent cover.

Finished Size

Any size

Materials

- Hessian/burlap fabric
- 100 percent cotton thread in a neutral color to match the fabric

Other Tools

- Curtain rod kit (if using as a curtain panel)
- Low-tack Velcro or extra strong if you don't mind removing the wall surface when you remove the headboard (if using as a headboard)
- Long ruler—at least 24in. long
- Tailor's chalk or dressmaker's pencil
- Fabric scissors
- Iron and ironing board
- Sewing machine

Prepare

Measure the wall, window, or door that you want the panel to hang on.

As a Curtain Panel

Install your curtain rod kit and measure from the top of the rod to the floor. Take this measurement and add approx. 2in. to the length and ¾in. to the width.

Cut

Cut the hessian to the correct measurement.

Sew

Turn over ⅜in. on each of the sides, press, and stitch. Turn over 1½in. on the top of the panel to the wrong side, press, and stitch. Slide onto the curtain pole. Check for and trim any excess threads.

As a Headboard

Measure from the position on the wall you would like the headboard to start down to the floor. Then measure the width of the bed. Take this measurement and add approx. $1\frac{1}{2}$in. to the length and $\frac{3}{4}$in. to the width.

Cut

Cut the hessian to the correct measurement.

Sew

Turn over $\frac{3}{8}$in. on the left and right sides, press, and stitch. Turn over $1\frac{1}{2}$in. on the top of the panel to the wrong side, press, and stitch. Check for and trim any excess threads. ▣ Attach pairs of Velcro dots together and then stick one side to the back of the panel. Press the other side firmly to the wall, making sure that you keep the line even.

Design Thoughts

Any translucent or loosely woven fabric will work well for this project. Instead of a standard curtain rod you could use any form of pipe or substantial doweling as long as you have in mind a way to attach the curtain rod to the ceiling or wall. These panels work really well to divide up a work or play space, as much as they do to screen an unpleasant view. I also like the idea of using these as a hanging pinboard.

Re-Upholstered Chairs

Chairs are a quirk of Western society. Many countries, such as Persia, India, and Japan, didn't feel the need for them. Even in the West, chairs were simply used as a way of expressing status until the 18th century. Comfort and conversation were not important.

Now the chair plays a central role in our lives. We need a chair for eating and a different chair for working. Most importantly, we need a chair for socializing and relaxing. Chairs have become a conduit to successful gatherings, meetings, and intimate conversations, which is why we always find room to squeeze another one somewhere into our home.

Chairs are built for one, but often look out of place alone. So we group them in pairs, or around a sofa or table, so that the chair becomes the catalyst for conversation.

Many of us harbor a desire to do a bit of upholstering. Small chairs or stools are the perfect starting point and repainting and upholstering them is not difficult. This is a great project to use vintage or ethnic textiles on as they add another layer of texture and pattern to your home without it becoming overwhelming.

Finished Size

- Look for a chair (or chairs) with good proportions and a sound structure. You may already have a chair waiting to be revitalized but, if not, buying a single chair from a market or fair is far more cost-effective than buying a pair. You can unify two different chairs by using the same fabric and paint colors.
- Use either a dining or bedroom chair for this with a drop-in seat. You will only need a small amount of fabric so you can use vintage, antique, or ethnic fabrics that may be cost-prohibitive on larger chairs.

Materials

- A chair or two
- Enough fabric to cover the seat. Measure the current upholstered section of the chair and add 6in. to each side.

Other Tools

- Pliers
- Staple gun or hammer and upholstery tacks
- Fabric scissors

If painting or waxing the chair

- Wire wool
- Fine sandpaper
- Paintbrush(es)
- Eggshell or gloss paint in a color of your choice and matching wood undercoat/primer OR furniture wax in a color of your choice.

Prepare

Remove the seat from your chair frame by unscrewing the screws on the underside, if it has them, or by simply lifting the seat out.

Painting or Waxing

If you are repainting or waxing the chair, you need to remove any wax or varnish with wire wool. If waxing, you need to totally remove the previous finish. If painting, you need to sand the wood enough to give it a "key." This means that new paint will adhere to the chair rather than chip and scratch. ▣ If painting, paint the chair with a thin layer of undercoat/primer. Watch for drips and make sure you paint the underside as well. Let dry for 2–4 hours, until it hardens completely. I also paint a second undercoat as this gives a better finish. Lightly sand between coats. Repeat with two layers of top coat, sanding between layers and leaving the required drying time. These layers make a big difference to the longevity of the finish. ▣ If waxing, follow the instructions on the packaging for the best finish.

Upholster

Using the pliers, strip all of the old fabric. ▣ If you're working with a fabric that has a pattern or a central motif, decide where you'd like it placed on the seat. It is best to place the top of the pattern at the back of the seat and the bottom of the pattern at the front of the seat. ▣ Staple or tack the fabric to the underside of the back of the seat. Once you've stapled the back, move on to the front. Then staple the right and left sides. Keep the fabric tight as you move around the seat. ▣ Make a pleat in every corner by pulling the fabric from the sides around to the front and back. Fold under enough of the excess fabric to make the edges of the folds flush with the corners. Cut out any excess fabric if you're having trouble getting it all folded under the pleats. ▣ Once you're happy with where your fabric is positioned, add in some extra staples or tacks to make sure all the fabric is held down tightly.

Trim any excess fabric away. Screw or put your seat back into the chair, and you're done.

Design Thoughts

For the chair shown here, I have used Kuba cloth from the Congo in Africa. It's a similar type of fabric to linen as it is handwoven using strands of raffia palm leaves. It's very labor intensive to make and therefore quite expensive. It is hand-dyed and has a wonderful "handle" to it, so I thought a chair would be an excellent place for it. Small pieces of special textiles work well for this project, so hunt out fabrics at antique or textile fairs to create something unique. You can unify a group of disparate chairs by using the same fabric (and paint or wax). Or you could make a set of chairs look more relaxed by using a different fabric on each chair.

Hemp Napkins

Hemp could have been made for napkins. It's extremely hardy but the more you use and wash it, the softer and lovelier it becomes. On a practical level, hemp is both antibacterial and stain-resistant, but from a purely aesthetic point of view, it is a visual and tactile delight. These napkins are simple and quick to make—you could banish paper napkins forever by rustling up a dozen or so. They make great housewarming gifts and they're the perfect project to reuse vintage hemp sheets that might be past their best for their original purpose.

Finished Size

- 19in. × 19in.
- Seam allowances are ⅜in. and are included in the cutting sizes.

Materials

- You can use new hemp fabric, or choose from vintage hemp products such as grain sacks, sheets, or cart covers. You can also buy rolls of vintage hemp. These are usually hand-loomed and are 48–24in. wide. You can adjust the size of your napkins to accommodate this if necessary.
- You will need a 20in. square per napkin. You can cut four napkins from just over a yard of hemp fabric, or approx. 12–16 from a vintage hemp sheet.
- 100 percent cotton thread in a neutral color—make sure you match the tone of the fabric as hemp runs from cream to oatmeal in color.

Other Tools

- Iron and ironing board
- Long ruler—at least 24in. long
- Tailor's chalk or dressmaker's pencil
- Fabric scissors
- Pins
- Sewing machine

Prepare

Prewash the fabric on a warm wash to eliminate any shrinkage. Dry, then press with a hot iron.

Cut

Decide on the number of napkins that you would like to make. Measure and mark 21¼in. squares onto the wrong side of your fabric. Then cut out your squares.

Sew

Use tailor's chalk or a pencil to mark a line ¾in. in from all four edges. Press two opposite edges in ⅜in. to meet the penciled line. Fold these folds over ¾in. once more, encasing the raw edges. Press and pin the folded edges. Starting approx. ¾in. from the corner, sew the two folds into place on your sewing machine, sewing close to the folded edge. Stop at the opposite intersecting drawn line, approx. 1¼in. from the raw edge. Repeat these steps for the remaining two edges. Fold all four corners into a triangle shape and press.

Slip stitch the corners closed, and your napkin is complete.

Design Thoughts

You can change the size of the napkins if you want to make them larger, or to incorporate a slightly smaller vintage piece of hemp fabric.

Use striped hemp or organically dyed hemp if you would like different-colored napkins (just make sure they are dye-fast). You could also adapt this idea to either vintage or new linen (but hemp is best).

Linen Comforter Cover and Pillowcases

It's not easy to get our necessary dose of sleep. Research tells us we sleep one and a half hours less each night than we did at the beginning of the century. We also don't experience the same extremes of seasonal changes in light and darkness, so our quality of sleep has deteriorated even further. This isn't good.

The bedroom has become the most important room in the home, for if we sleep less, and less effectively, we need to make the environment as comforting as possible. You want your bedroom to be quiet, cool, and well ventilated. You definitely want it free of synthetic fabrics. They don't breathe like cotton and linen, which means you can wake up with something akin to a hangover. They also don't feel very nice.

Sheets should be a daily delight—good bed linen makes a difference to how you sleep and, therefore, how you feel. Linen is best—it doesn't retain moisture as cotton does, is cool in summer, and will last forever. As a last word, that same research tells us that linen bedding helps people get to sleep much faster and results in a deeper and more refreshing night's sleep.

So, wrap yourself, center yourself, and sleep well, nestled in your linen bedding.

Finished Size

- Double comforter cover $78^3/_4$in. × $78^3/_4$in.
- Queen comforter cover $88^1/_2$in. × $86^1/_2$in.
- Pillowcases   20in. × $29^1/_2$in
- Seam allowances are $^3/_8$in. and are included in the cutting sizes.

Materials

- Linen fabric—either vintage or antique sheets, or new linen off the roll. You can buy linen in various widths—some up to 118in. wide, but most will be 54in. in width. The width of the fabric you choose will determine the amount of fabric you will need to buy, as you may need to join two pieces of fabric together to create the required width.
- 100 percent cotton thread in a color to match the fabric—linen can be white, cream, or ecru in tone.

Other Tools

- Iron and ironing board
- Long ruler—at least 24in. long
- Tailor's chalk or dressmaker's pencil
- Fabric scissors
- Pins
- Sewing machine

Prepare

Prewash the fabric on a warm wash to eliminate any shrinkage. Dry, then press with a hot iron.

Cut

- Double: Cut either two pieces at $79^1/_2$in. × $82^1/_4$in. or four pieces at 40in. × $82^1/_4$in.
- Queen: Cut either two pieces at $89^1/_2$in. × $90^1/_4$in. or four pieces at 45in. × $90^1/_4$in.
- Pillowcases: Cut two pieces at $20^1/_2$in. × $30^3/_4$in. and two pieces at $20^1/_2$in. × 37in. to make two pillowcases.

Sew the comforter cover

If you need to join two pieces together to make the full width, pin two pieces of linen together, right sides facing, down the long edge. Sew together and press the seams flat with a hot iron. Topstitch down both sides of the center line. Repeat for the remaining two pieces. You now have two complete panels. ◨ Then, on your bottom edge of one panel, fold over and press 1½in. toward the wrong side of the fabric. Fold over and press another 1½in. toward the wrong side. Pin and topstitch along both edges. Repeat for the second panel. ◨ Pin the two panels together around the three raw edges, with right sides facing. Sew a ⅜in. seam around the three edges and either serge or zigzag the raw edges. Press the seams and clip the corners. Turn right side out and press again. ◨ Your comforter closures can be buttons and buttonholes or snaps (or a mixture). I have used snaps on the inside and then sewn a button on the outside, so that it looks smarter.

Sew the pillowcases

On all four pieces, fold over and press ⅜in. toward the wrong side of the fabric, on one of the shorter edges. Fold over and press another ⅜in. toward the wrong side. Pin and topstitch along the edge. Serge or zigzag the three raw edges. ◨ To make an envelope closure, lay one long piece down with the right side facing up and the topstitched edge to the left. Lay the shorter piece on top of this, with the right side facing down and matching the raw edges. The topstitched edge should also be to the left. ◨ Fold the extra fabric from the longer piece back over the top of the shorter piece so that the shorter piece edge meets the fold line. ◨ Pin and stitch around the three serged edges. Press the seams and clip the corners. Turn right side out and press again. Repeat for the second pillowcase.

You might need a little nap now. . .

Design Thoughts

You can use almost any linen fabric for bed linen, but a medium-weight one is best. Vintage linen sheets would be fantastic to use and are very simple to work with, as sheets are always bigger than comforter covers. Try to match the tones of vintage cloth as they can often be slightly different.

Any color of linen or any patterned linen would be suitable, but if you need to join fabrics, make sure that any patterns meet correctly.

You can use a contrast thread for the topstitch and could add your own embroidery or monogram. This bed linen is an investment and will be with you for a long time, so it's the perfect project to make very personal.

Hand-Dyed Linen Pillows

Sometimes you want a pillow that is simple—restrained, subtle, and comforting. Nothing that is terribly "now" or this season, but a piece that you'll keep for a long time. A mainstay that can be the backdrop to some Liberty print pillows or any pillow using a patterned textile. Plain pillows need a little "3-D-ness" to keep them from looking too plain, so I often use handwoven fabrics to balance this out. They are usually very textured and can be fine, such as the ramie linen I used for this project, or chunky, such as feedsacks or cart cloths.

The cloth itself has already been created by a pair of human hands rather than a machine, so the touch of the maker is apparent. I always think that a home needs a little of the handmade to make it feel lived in and comforting and to balance out the necessary mass-produced items.

With the use of vegetable dyes, the linen then seems to take on another dimension—a kind of depth and subtlety that commercial dyes can't reproduce.

But the best thing about making these pillows is that the effort required to make them is so much less than the reward.

Finished Size

- 20in. × 20in.
- Seam allowances are ⅜in. and are included in the cutting sizes.

Materials

- You will need 21½in. loosely woven white linen—I have used ramie, but a shirting weight or gauze would also be good.
- 100 percent cotton thread in white

Other tools

- Iron and ironing board
- Long ruler—at least 24in. long
- Tailor's chalk or dressmaker's pencil
- Fabric scissors
- Pins
- Sewing machine
- 20in. feather and down pillow form per pillow
- Natural dye—see pages 15–17.

Prepare

Prewash the fabric on a warm wash to eliminate any shrinkage. Dry, then press with a hot iron.

Cut

For each pillow, on the wrong side of the fabric, measure, and mark 20½in. × 20½in. squares—two for each pillow. Then cut out.

Sew

Pin the two squares together with right sides facing. Sew around three sides and approx. 4in. on each end of the fourth side, so that you have an opening for the pillow form. It's important to use 100 percent cotton thread, as polyester thread won't pick up the dye so well.
- Press the seams open and trim the corners. - Turn the pillow right side out and gently push out the corners to make them nice and sharp.

Dye

Now the fun bit! Go to pages 15–17 to read through the section on natural dyes. Choose your leaf, tea, or powdered dye and dye the pillow outer as instructed.

Finishing

Once the cover is dyed and dried, give it a quick wash in a delicate or handwash detergent. I just swill it around in a bucket with some handwash detergent and then rinse it under the tap. This is to get rid of any excess dye. Once it is dry again, press with a hot iron and slip your pillow insert inside. ⊡ Slip-stitch the opening closed with the thread color of your choice. I promise you won't ever view a "plain" pillow in the same way.

Design Thoughts

Different natural dye colors usually complement each other beautifully—a little like nature itself. Think about leaves with flowers, or bark with berries. Take the opportunity to dye a batch of pillows in different colors.

You can change the size of the pillows—they would be a stunning addition as large bedroom pillows.

I used an Indian antique gold thread to stitch my pillows closed. You can use a contrasting or a similar color, embellish with brocade or ribbon, and, of course, use different weight linens if you prefer. Vintage Hungarian feedsacks would be amazing hand-dyed. They absorb the color more densely, leaving the resulting color saturated rather than almost luminous.

If you are clever with your sewing, pop in a zipper—just make sure you purchase a "dye-able" cotton zipper.

Your choices are endless, but they will all be lovely.

The Senses

We are born with five (some say six) senses, with touch being our first to develop and the most important, physically and emotionally.

When looking for fabric, we are always drawn by the eye first—usually the color speaks to us and then the pattern. The clashing vibrant prints of India thrill some of us, while the muted palette of southern France lights up others. You may like plain, patterned, floral, or striped—bold contrasts or none at all. Find the look of the fabric that you love, but don't stop there: Feel it—this is vital. If you're going to sleep under it, rest on it, or wear it, it has to feel good and natural cloth always feels best.

When we touch something, we connect with it. Looking at something is often a detached observation but you cannot be detached when you touch it. Lack of sensory stimulation often makes us sad or anxious, so it is important to make sure your home (your nest) is full of tactile pleasures. Wool blankets comfort us with their weight and warmth. Silk pillows sooth us. We make seasonal changes by changing from linen to leather and silk to wool as we adapt our homes to shelter and cosset us through sun, rain, and snow.

Books and Magazines

These are the books and magazines I refer to again and again. Some are very specific (and facts and figures based). Others are very much a visual feast, while some are a mixture of both.

Books

Textiles: A World Tour—Catherine Legrand

Textile Style: Decorating with Antique and Exotic Fabrics—Caroline Clifton-Mogg

Fabric Inspirations—Kate French and Katherine Sorrell

Second Skin: Choosing and Caring for Textiles and Clothing—India Flint

Eco Color: Botanical Dyes for Beautiful Textiles—India Flint

Textiles: The Art of Mankind—Mary Schoeser

World Textiles: A Visual Guide to Traditional Techniques—John Gillow and Bryan Sentence

Home is Where the Heart is?—Ilse Crawford

Etcetera—Creating Beautiful Interiors with the Things You Love—Sibella Court

Nomad—Bringing Your Travels Home—Sibella Court

Unwrapped—Carolyn Quartermaine

Indigo: Egyptian Mummies to Blue Jeans—Jenny Balfour-Paul

Celia Birtwell—Celia Birtwell

Florence Broadhurst: Her Secret & Extraordinary Lives—Helen O'Neill

Handmade Home: Living with Art and Craft—Mark & Sally Bailey

Quilting, Patchwork & Appliqué: A World Guide—Caroline Crabtree and Christine Shaw

William Morris Textiles—Linda Parry

Textile Designers at the Cutting Edge—Bradley Quinn

Madeleine Vionnet—Betty Kirke

Classic and Modern Fabrics: The Complete Illustrated Sourcebook—Janet Wilson

Magazines

Not many—but I think all you need for inspiration.

Elle Décor (U.S.A.) www.elledecor.com

Hand/Eye (U.S.A.) www.handeyemagazine.com

Selvedge (U.K.) www.selvedge.org

The World of Interiors (U.K.) www.worldofinteriors.co.uk

Museums and Galleries

The museums and galleries listed either specialize in textiles or have significant galleries dedicated to the craft of cloth. Look at their websites as well, as many have online resources.

North America

THE METROPOLITAN
MUSEUM OF ART
1000 Fifth Avenue
New York
NY 10028–0198
U.S.A.

THE CLOISTERS
MUSEUM AND
GARDENS
99 Margaret Corbin
Drive
Fort Tryon Park
New York
NY 10040
U.S.A.
www.metmuseum.org

TEXTILE MUSEUM
2320 S. Street, N.W.
Washington DC
20008–4008
U.S.A.
www.textilemuseum.org

TEXTILE MUSEUM OF
CANADA
55 Center Avenue
Toronto, Ontario
M5G 2H5
Canada
www.textilemuseum.ca

Europe

THE VICTORIA AND
ALBERT MUSEUM
Cromwell Road
South Kensington
London
SW7 2RL
England
www.vam.ac.uk

BRITISH MUSEUM
Great Russell Street
London
WC1B 3DG
England
www.britishmuseum.org

MUSÉE DES TISSUS ET
DES ARTS DÉCORATIFS
34 Rue de la Charité
69002 Lyon
France
www.musee-des-tissus.com

Australasia

NATIONAL TEXTILE
MUSEUM OF AUSTRALIA
Urrbrae House
Fullarton Road
Urrbrae
Adelaide
South Australia 5064
Australia

TE PAPA
55 Cable Street
Te Aro
Wellington 6140
New Zealand
www.tepapa.govt.nz

Asia

THE CALICO MUSEUM
OF TEXTILES
Sarabhai Foundation
opposite Underbridge
Shahibag
Ahmedabad
Gujarat 380004
India

MUSEE DE SOME
SEIRYU (MUSEUM OF
DYEING)
Meirin-biru 6th floor
550-1
Yamabushiyama-cho,
550-1
Muromachi-dori Nishiki
Koji Agaru
Nakagyo-ku
Kyoto City
Japan 604–8156
*http://www.someseiryu.
net/e_index.html*

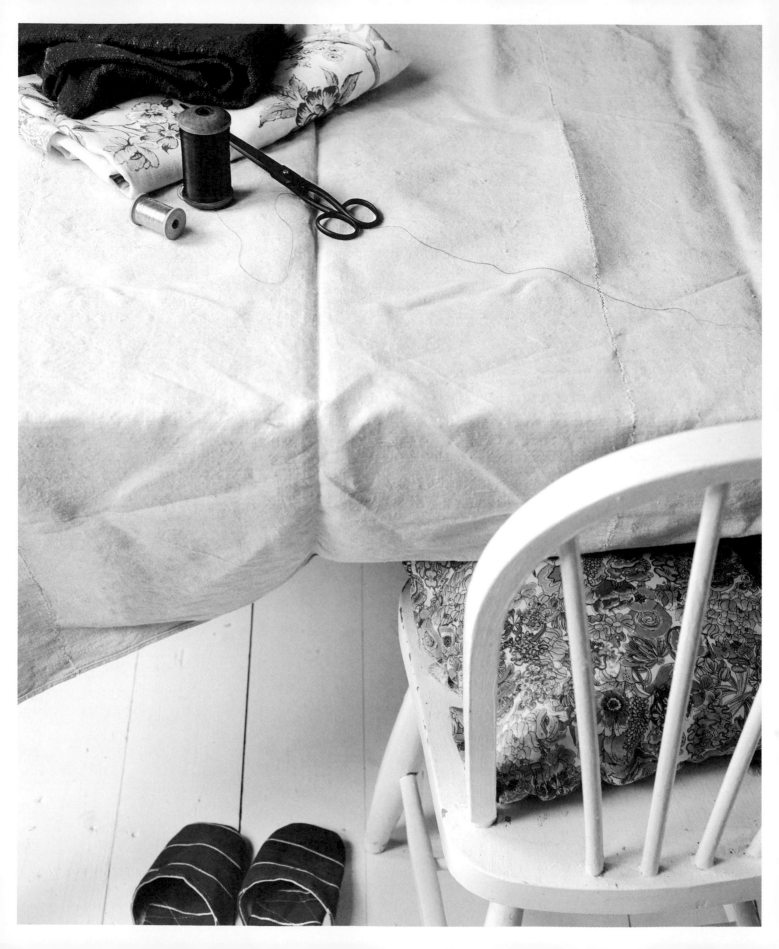

Online Sources

Fabric

www.africanfabric.co.uk
The best source for African fabrics. Magie Relph knows her stuff and the fabrics are very reasonably priced.

www.alabamachanin.com
A wonderful high-end bespoke and D.I.Y. design company headed by Natalie Chanin. Her online journal is a source of really interesting ideas that make you think (very hard) about the role cloth and making have in our lives.

www.anansevillage.com
Fairtrade African fabrics.

www.beckfordsilk.co.uk
For a great range of undyed silks.

www.bishopstontrading.co.uk
An excellent selection of organic fabrics.

www.clothaholics.com
For Japanese indigo cottons and vintage kimonos.

www.etsy.com and *www.folksy.com*
Both are excellent resources for antique and vintage cloth as well as new cloth from around the world. Lots of specialist ethnic fabric suppliers, as well as individual designers.

www.filzfelt.com
Felt nirvana.

www.foglinenwork.com/en
Simple linen homewares and accessories from Japan.

www.habutextiles.com
Incredible selection of Japanese wool, silk, and cotton.

www.ichiroya.com
Antique and vintage Japanese cloth and kimonos.

www.kimonoboy.com
Japanese folk textiles.

www.lavivahome.com
An amazing and very personal selection of ethnic textiles.

www.leprevo.co.uk
A very helpful small company for all your leather needs—no order is too small and they are happy to send samples. They don't have an online store, but you can browse everything online.

www.lesindiennes.com
Beautiful hand-block-printed cottons that you can order in 5 yd bolts.

www.linjong.com
Traditionally made textiles from Thailand and other countries in Southeast Asia.

www.lin-net.com/English/shop_linnen.html
Another lovely—slightly more feminine—Japanese textile offering.

www.londonclothcompany.com
A microweaving company based in London. Mostly wool, but all lovely.

www.organiccotton.biz
I get lots of fabric from here. They have a great selection and are really passionate about their business and organic cotton.

www.parna.co.uk
The best source of vintage hemp and linen that I have found online.

www.sallycampbell.com.au
A stunning range of vintage and handmade textiles from India.

www.stjudesfabrics.co.uk
St Jude's makes and sells unique fabrics and wallpapers, working with an eclectic range of artists to produce U.K.-printed fabrics. My favorites are by Mark Hearld.

www.uzbek-craft.com
Ikat and Suzani fabric.

Natural Dyes

You can raid the produce section of your local grocery store or market to create natural dyes, but if you would like to try powdered dyes, here are three good sources:

www.naturaldyes.co.uk
www.naturaldyes.org
www.wildcolors.co.uk

Haberdashery and Handles

www.merchantandmills.com
All the haberdashery you could want, all very nicely packaged including leather handle kits.

www.theidentitystore.co.uk
This company sells leather as well as the tools and hardware needed for the leather projects.

www.u-handbag.com
Almost everything you need to make a bag, including handle kits.

Stores and Markets

U.S.A.

ABC CARPET & HOME
888 & 881 Broadway
East 19th Street
New York, NY 10003
www.abchome.com
Ten floors offering an
inspired collection of rugs,
furniture, antiques, home
textiles, accessories, and
sustainable furnishings.

B&J FABRICS
525 7th Avenue
New York, NY 10018
www.bandjfabrics.com
This fabric emporium's
extensive online store makes
up only a small fraction
of their beautiful, well-
organized collection of
fabrics in-store.

ELFRIEDE'S FINE FABRICS
2425 Canyon Boulevard
Boulder, CO 80302
www.elfriedesfinefabrics.com
A source for unique and
extraordinary garment
and quilting fabrics.

F AND S FABRICS
10629 West Pico
Boulevard
Los Angeles, CA 90064
www.fandsfabrics.com
An eclectic mix of high
design textiles and trims,
with a wide array of color
and textural options.

FANCY TIGER CRAFTS
59 Broadway
Denver, CO 80203
www.fancytiger.com
A well-curated DIY
boutique featuring organic
cottons and eco-friendly
and socially conscious yarns.

MOOD DESIGNER FABRICS
225 W 37th Street
3rd Floor
New York, NY 10018
www.moodfabrics.com
The number-one shopping
destination for fashion fabric
in the world: The NYC
flagship store alone plays
host to more than 1,200
customers every day.

PURL SOHO
459 Broome Sreet
New York, NY 10013
www.purlsoho.com
A super fabric and yarn shop.
They sell almost all their
products online and curate
their products very well.

TEXTILE FABRICS
2717 Franklin Park
Nashville, TN 37204
www.textilefabricstore.com
Their 10,000 square foot
showroom is stocked with
a large range of natural
fabrics.

A VERB FOR KEEPING WARM
6328 San Pablo Avenue
Oakland, CA 94608
*www.averbforkeepingwarm.
com*
Unique, high-quality
fiber, yarn, dyes, and
spinning equipment.
This is a great place to
find local textiles dyed
with organic, sustainably
harvested extracts.

U.K.

CABBAGES & ROSES
3 Langton Street
Chelsea
London
SW10 0JL
www.cabbagesandroses.com
Simple fabrics all printed
in England.

CELIA BIRTWELL
Unit 5, Baseline
Business Studios
Whitchurch Road
London
W11 4TT
www.celiabirtwell.com
I have a huge soft spot for
Celia Birtwell fabrics. Just
the right amount of whimsy,
as well as perfect palettes.

CLOTH HOUSE
47 Berwick Street
London
W1F 8SJ
and 98 Berwick Street
London
W1F 0QJ
www.clothhouse.com
Cloth House fabrics come
from around the world. The
owners work closely with
the local textile traders and
craftspeople in order to
support them locally and to
maintain traditional skills.

THE CLOTH SHOP
290 Portobello Road
London
W10 5TE
www.theclothshop.net
The Cloth Shop is an
Aladdin's cave of intriguing
fabric and cloth, including
antique Swedish rag
rugs, Indian silk shawls,
cashmere and wool blankets
from Scotland, and antique
Welsh blankets.

EGG
36 Kinnerton Street
London
SW1X 8ES
www.eggtrading.com
My favorite store in London.
The store is merchandized
beautifully and sells
clothing and accessories as
well as artisan installations.

IAN MANKIN
271–273 Wandsworth
Bridge Road
London
SW6 2TX
www.ianmankin.co.uk
Ian Mankin has been
producing beautifully simple
cloth since the early 1980s.
Their fabrics are made from
100 percent natural fibers,
and over 90 percent are
woven in England.

JEN JONES
Pontbrendu
Llanybydder
Ceredigion
SA40 9UJ
www.jen-jones.com
Quite simply the largest
collection and stock of
antique Welsh quilts and
Welsh blankets anywhere
in the world.

JOSS GRAHAM
10 Eccleston Street
London
SW1W 9LT
www.jossgraham.com
Specializing in traditional
textiles and costume from
the Indian subcontinent,
central Asia, Tibet, and
north and west Africa.

LIBERTY LONDON
Regent Street
London
W1B 5AH
www.liberty.co.uk
For Liberty fabric, of course,
but also for Kaffe Fassett
cloth and a small selection
of other Rowan fabrics.

MELIN TREGWYNT
Castlemorris
Haverfordwest
Pembrokeshire
SA62 5UX
www.melintregwynt.co.uk
A favorite for Welsh wools—as
fabric or made into blankets,
pillows, and other accessories.

SELVEDGE
162 Archway Road
London
N6 5BB
www.selvedge.org
Lovely artisan textile goods,
plus a good selection of books.

TINSMITHS
Tinsmiths Alley
8A High Street
Ledbury
Herefordshire
HR8 1DS
www.tinsmiths.co.uk
Tinsmiths stock lovely natural
cottons and linens from a very
well-selected range including
St Jude's.

TIMOROUS BEASTIES
384 Great Western Road
Glasgow
G4 9HT
or 46 Amwell Street
London
EC1R 1XS
www.timorousbeasties.com
Slightly surreal but definitely
fantastic fabrics.

TOBIAS AND THE ANGEL
68 White Hart Lane
London
SW13 0PZ
An icon in London, Angel
carries her own hand-
printed fabric as well as
an extensive collection of
antique and vintage finds.

VV ROULEAUX
102 Marylebone Lane
London
W1U 2QD
www.vvrouleaux.com
Another iconic store for all
your passementerie needs.

Interesting Organizations and People

AID TO ARTISANS *www.aidtoartisans.org*
Aid to Artisans creates economic opportunities for artisan groups in which livelihoods, communities, and craft traditions are marginal or at risk. They connect businesses with artisans and work with them to help long-term economic growth as well as making very desirable products.

DOSA *www.dosainc.com*
Christina Kim of Dosa is widely regarded as a fabric visionary. She has spent over 20 years with artisans around the world forging ongoing relationships with indigenous craftspeople. Her company makes extraordinary clothing and homewares while creating industry and income for those that need it.

FIBERCOPIA *www.fibercopia.com*
A simple but very informative blog on textile designers, products, and producers.

FINE CELL WORK *www.finecellwork.co.uk*
Fine Cell Work is a social enterprise that trains prisoners in paid, skilled, creative needlework undertaken in the long hours spent in their cells to foster hope, discipline, and self-esteem.

THE HARRIS TWEED AUTHORITY *www.harristweed.org*
The "guardians of the orb." An excellent information source on Harris Tweed, with links to mills and small producers.

HEARTWEAR *www.edelkoort.com/heartwear*
Heartwear is a nonprofit organization that collaborates with artisans by helping them to produce their products on a larger scale, without compromising their know-how, skills, culture, or the environment in which they live and work.

KIRSTEN HECKERMANN *www.kirstenhecktermann.com*
Kirsten creates stunning hand dyed cotton velvet fabric and pillows.

MAGGIE GALTON *www.maggiegalton.com*
Maggie Galton works with artisans in indigenous and Mestizo communities throughout Mexico to revive dying craft traditions and develop new products that strike a balance between modernity and traditional tastes.

MOLLOY & SONS *http://molloyandsons.com*
Revered for the color, beauty, and quality of their wool tweeds, Molloy & Sons are one of the few companies who can proudly claim to create authentic Donegal tweed. Recently reinvigorated, their wonderful wool is traversing the globe.

ROSE DE BORMAN *www.rdeborman.co.uk*
London-based Rose de Borman paints and prints exquisite textiles by hand.

SELF-EMPLOYED WOMEN'S ASSOCIATION (SEWA)
www.sewa.org
SEWA is the largest union in India and is composed entirely of women. It works with small cooperatives of craftswomen to secure and build small businesses so that they are able to support their families with full employment as well as benefits.

TEXTILE EXCHANGE *http://textileexchange.org*
Textile Exchange is a nonprofit organization that equips people to accelerate sustainable practices in the textile value chain. In partnership with farmers, manufacturers, brands and retailers, they helped the organic cotton market grow from $240 million in 2001 to $6.8 billion in 2011.

THE TEXTILE SOCIETY *www.textilesociety.org.uk*
The Textile Society promotes the study of textile disciplines and celebrates the history and culture of textiles. They offer support to students, designers, historians, and practitioners through their educational and professional awards, as well as hosting regular textile fairs.

THREADS OF LIFE *www.threadsoflife.com*
Threads of Life are a Fairtrade business aiming to alleviate poverty in rural Indonesia. Heirloom-quality textiles and baskets are made with local materials and natural dyes. With the proceeds from their gallery, they help weavers form independent cooperatives and manage resources sustainably.

TINA TABONE *www.tinatabone.com*
Tina Tabone is a social anthropologist and peripatetic dealer in traditional textile art. She sells textiles that she acquires on her travels throughout the world, taking care that each piece is authentic and is part of the textile tradition of the culture in which it was produced.

Index

Acknowledgments

Cloth was a true collaboration and it is all the better for it.

Thank you, Cath, for the most wonderful photographs. You "see" textiles like no one else and brought everything to life so beautifully, for which I'm really grateful. You also make me laugh—a lot—for which I'm especially grateful, because I know how serious I can be.

To my editor, Vicky—thank you first of all for making this so easy and for being so delightful and supportive to be with. I love this book and that's because you helped me do it how I saw it and I can't tell you how much I appreciate that.

To the very talented Laurie-Ann. You are a truly gifted book designer and you have made *Cloth* very beautiful—thank you.

Thank you, Sara, for smoothing out my sometimes overexcited words. It's so much better for your eyes and edit.

Thank you, Kyle. You gave me the opportunity to create *Cloth* as well as a wonderful team to work with, for which I am truly thankful.

Some wonderful people and companies lent their products to tell the story of cloth. Thank you Magie from African Fabrics and Kath from Parna Textiles. Both incredible textile experts who source exquisite cloth. Thank you, Lewis & Wood, for providing incredible British cloth. I know it isn't easy to manufacture like you do, but it is worth it.—and your fabrics are beautiful. Thank you, Carolyn and Roderick from Merchant & Mills for providing the very best in haberdashery—the book is so much better for your relentless search for the best. And thank you, Billy Lloyd, for your pots—they are truly special.

To my friends and family—I'm sorry for my lengthy distractions and disappearances, but thank you so much for your words of encouragement and support. To Lily and Mr. Darcy—so sorry for the shorter walks and late dinners, but a big thank you for gracing us with your presence on these pages and for being such funny company on shoot days.

To Ed—Thank you and thank you.

Published in 2014 by
Stewart, Tabori & Chang
An imprint of ABRAMS

First published in Great Britain by Kyle Books in 2013

Text © 2013 Cassandra Ellis
Photographs © 2013 Catherine Grathwicke
Design © 2013 Kyle Books
Illustrations (Page 49) © 2013 Esther Coombs

Library of Congress Control Number: 2013950194
ISBN: 978-1-61769-109-6

Editors, STC edition: Cristina Garces and Melanie Falick
Cover Design, STC edition: Deb Wood
Production Manager, STC edition: Erin Vandeveer
Editor: Vicky Orchard
Designer: Laurie-Ann Ward

Printed and bound in China
10 9 8 7 6 5 4 3 2 1

Stewart, Tabori & Chang books are available at special discounts when purchased in quantity for premiums and promotions as well as fundraising or educational use. Special editions can also be created to specification. For details, contact specialsales@abramsbooks.com or the address below.

115 West 18th Street
New York, NY 10011
www.abramsbooks.com

5819

5819